A WELL-KEPT HOME

Household Traditions and Simple

Secrets from a French Grandmother

First published in the United States of America in 2001
by Universe Publishing
A Division of Rizzoli International Publications, Inc
300 Park Avenue South
New York NY 10010

ISBN 0-7893-0528-3

Original title : LES SECRETS DE GRAND-MÈRE
Written and designed by : Laura Fronty
Photographs by : Yves Duronsoy
Published by Les Editions du Chêne - Hachette Livre 1999

01 02 03 04 05 / 10 9 8 7 6 5 4 3 2 1

Printed in France

A WELL-KEPT HOME

HOUSEHOLD TRADITIONS AND SIMPLE

SECRETS FROM A FRENCH GRANDMOTHER

Text

LAURA FRONTY

Photographs

YVES DURONSOY

UNIVERSE

To our Grandmothers
Lila and Albertine

CONTENTS

INTRODUCTION 9

FOR THE GASTRONOME
Back from the market 13
Food preservation 25
Butter, eggs, cheese and milk 37
Cake-making hints and tips 47

HOME SWEET HOME
Traditional paints 53
Light 57
Perfumes and scents 67
Flowers and bouquets 71
Furniture, wooden and parquet floors 79
Sparkling tableware 83
Clean and beautiful 91

THE LINEN CUPBOARD
Washing, drying and ironing 101
Traditional dyes 109
Clothes and accessories 111

BEAUTY AND WELL-BEING
Health through plants 121
Refined toiletries 125
Perfumes and lotions 133

BACK TO NATURE
Roses and rosebushes 139
Sowing and repotting 143
Protecting plants 147
The gardener's tools 152

BASIC PRODUCTS TO USE AT HOME 155
RECIPE LIST AND INDEX 157
ACKNOWLEDGEMENTS 159

Introduction

Memories of my childhood, of houses and places, merge together in my mind to form a single composition. I remember how the floor of my childhood home was washed with soap like the deck of a boat and how we used to run barefoot upon it. The main entrance was dark, the study crimson, but everywhere else pure white dominated. Large ecru linen curtains filtered the falling light and jewels decorated the walls like branches…

This was a house dedicated to writing: a variety of pots held all sorts of pens, pencils and erasers, but there was only one sort of ink available: green, the color of hope. It was here that books ruled supreme: they climbed to the ceiling, piled up at the foot of our beds and invaded every space.

The scent of geranium, tuberose and sandalwood floated in the air. We bought *grasse* essences in aluminium flasks corked with red wax. By mixing these essences together, we created our own personal scents, which we sometimes burned on naked flames.

The kitchen was always a place suffused with the aroma of herbs, chillies, spices, fruits and blackberry jam. It housed collections of earthenware from Provence, Morocco and Spain, as well as mis-matched glasses. Meals prepared there always seemed to come from far away, even if in fact the recipes only came from Normandy, Burgundy or Lorraine.

The garden was the domain of both parents and children. We would bury garlic cloves at the foot of rosebushes to make them pinker. Even if the pumpkins that were grown there did not turn into carriages, they still seemed gigantic to me, especially since my grandfather knew a magical formula to make them grow faster! The morning in all its glory entwined itself around the arbor and shutters as the golden buttercups sprouted in the grass.

Summer was spent in Provence. Glass pebbles, gathered on the beach, would be transformed in winter into a stained-glass curtain embroidered with colorful trinkets, inspired by ancient Indian saris.

My childhood home belonged to a woman who found happiness in the simplest of tasks. She made taking a cold shower in the old washhouse a pleasurable experience using a jug decorated with naïve flowers to rinse us down. She hung lanterns in trees, like fireflies in the night, so as to make the darkness seem magical and scare away the wolves that might be hiding…

Every year she repainted the house with lime, which left white marks on visitors, but she was fascinated by the brilliant colors of India and Mexico, which she used as an inspiration to make clothes for me. To entice sweet dreams, she turned my bedroom ceiling into a light blue sky illuminated with golden stars in the same way as in a chapel. I was a princess in my bed protected by a mosquito net and my nights were filled with the scent of lemon balm which was poured into small cups dotted around the house to keep the insects away.

She could sew, embroider and mend an old fabric found in a flea market, but she was also capable of stripping back and renovating an old wardrobe.

Although refined and sophisticated, she favored simplicity and all things natural. It is therefore in remembrance of her and what I learned living in her presence that I have written this book.

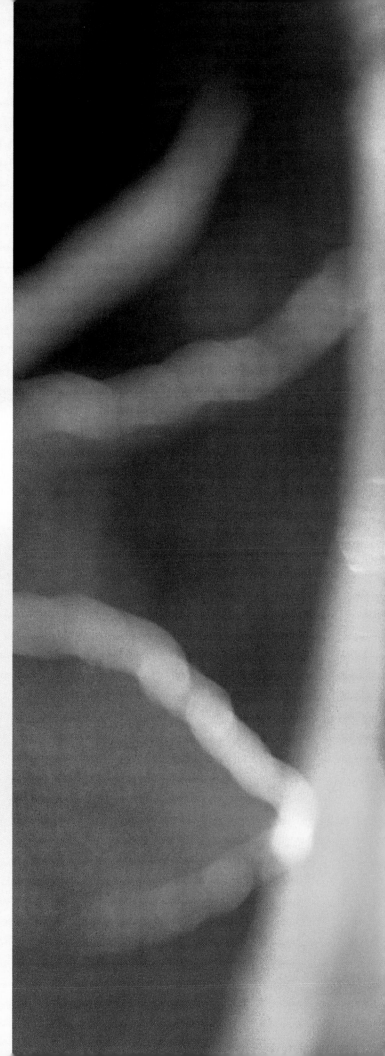

FOR THE
gastronome

*C*ooking is a source of great pleasure, both for those who do it and for those who taste its results, often stimulating emotions and sensations that date back to childhood. Each one of us has in a corner of our memory hidden flavors and smells that suddenly emerge at unexpected moments in our life. Fruits heating in a copper pan, filling the whole house with their aroma like nothing else; grated chocolate on buttered bread or traditionally whisked in a cup; the smell of toast and hot coffee in the morning: all these images can unlock a personal story whose secrets are known only to us.

Back from the market

❧ *In Paris, at the Saint-Germain market, there was a small lady dressed in a black satin smock, who sold produce from her tiny garden located a few kilometres from the capital. On her stall we found red lettuces, herbs, wild strawberries and raspberries in punnets covered in chestnut leaves to keep the fruit fresh. She also sold flowers that grew in her vegetable patch: small mossy roses as well as gigantic and flamboyant dahlias...*

Each year, when we went on holiday to the South, we marvelled at the markets of Vallauris or Antibes, filled with explosive colors and scents, and echoing with the cries of the market vendors. At that time it was only in Provençal markets that you came across courgette flowers, just in bloom, with which the people of Nice made delicious fritters. It was also in Provence that we sometimes ate salads that were spiced with orange, red or yellow nasturtiums, whose peppery taste was astonishing, or seasoned with sky-blue borage, which tasted like cucumber or fresh wheat grains...❧

Melon

❧ When you buy a melon, it must be heavy and firm. Feel its weight and pull gently on its stalk; a small green crown should appear when it is pulled off. Its smell should not be sickly as this would mean it is overripe.

Citrus fruits

For marmalades, liqueurs and other syrups, use only untreated varieties.

❧ To preserve lemons, put them in a bowl and cover them with fresh water, which should be changed regularly. This method, used in Morocco, makes the fruits juicier.

❧ Fruits will yield even more juice if you roll them vigorously under your hand before pressing.

LEFT-HAND PAGE
The piquancy of nasturtiums will spice up the mild flavor of lettuce while at the same time imparting color.

RIGHT-HAND PAGE
Once salted and jarred,
these preserved lemons are
suspended in olive oil and
flavored with herbs and spices:
pepper, chilli, garlic
or bay leaves are the
most appropriate.

Grapes, plums and mirabelles

These fruits often have the appearance of being covered with a sort of translucent frost, the correct term for which is pruina. The presence of this fragile powder attests to the freshness of the fruit.

Strawberries

∾ To avoid their becoming waterlogged, wash strawberries very briefly under running water before removing their stalks.

∾ If you find they lack flavor, add the juice and grated zest of a lemon, a pinch of ground pepper or a few chopped fresh mint leaves.

Cauliflower

The firm florets of a fresh cauliflower should be white and spotless and have no smell. In the same way as a melon should, this vegetable should feel heavy.

∾ In order to keep the florets white, add lemon juice to the cooking water.

∾ I have to admit that the piece of stale bread or French toast that our grandmothers put in the cooking water to combat the smell makes very little difference. The best way is simply to choose a very fresh cauliflower, keep the window open and avoid overcooking!

Lila's preserved lemons

1 KG (2¼ LB) SMALL UNTREATED LEMONS
(OR ENOUGH TO FILL THE JAR)
ABOUT 20 G (¾ OZ) COARSE SALT
2 SMALL CHILLIES
2 BAY LEAVES
PEPPER

1. Cut a deep cross down through each lemon, but without cutting all the way through the fruit.

2. Fill the openings with coarse salt.

3. Pack the lemons in a glass jar, previously sterilized by boiling.

4. Add the chillies, bay leaves and pepper. Cover the lemons with boiling water and any remaining coarse salt.

5. Leave to marinate for at least 3 weeks, before using these preserved lemons in a Moroccan tagine or to flavor a pork, chicken, rabbit or fish stew.

Artichokes

Artichoke leaves should be firm and really green. To check their freshness, fold back one of the leaves: if fresh, it will break neatly with a distinctive sound.

～ Small purple artichokes, also called "peppery artichokes", are eaten raw, with salt, *barigoule* (cooked in olive oil) or *farigoulette* style (*farigoulette* is the name for thyme in Provence).

～ Round artichokes should be eaten cooked. Before cooking them, break off the stalks so as to get rid of the maximum amount of fibre. The French tend to throw away these stalks, but in Spain, for example, they are peeled, cooked with the artichokes and then seasoned and finally eaten.

～ We sometimes forget that artichokes are actually flowers. If they are not picked, they will bloom into superb flowers of an intense mauve color. When they are picked as a vegetable, to prolong their lifespan treat them like fresh-cut flowers: immerse their stalks in fresh water in a vase or large glass, and remember to change the water daily.

～ However, remember that, once they are cooked, artichokes should always be eaten immediately; if they are kept, even in a fridge, they oxidize and become toxic.

Beans

When buying green beans, make a point of breaking a few in two. A good bean should break neatly with a crisp snap, and show no strings.

～ When preparing beans, it is best to string them by hand – when using a knife, it is all too easy to miss a few strings.

～ In order to retain their vibrant color, simply add half a teaspoonful of bicarbonate of soda to the cooking water and do not cover during cooking (this advice also applies to peas).

～ You can preserve green beans by alternating a layer of beans and a layer of coarse salt in a stoneware pot. Before cooking them, it is absolutely essential to rinse them thoroughly in clean cold water in order to get rid of the excess salt.

～ To keep the beans crunchy (for example in a salad), rinse them quickly under cold running water immediately after cooking.

～ *Coco rose* (pink-veined) beans should be really pink and have no reddish marks. Similarly, wax beans should be bright yellow.

LEFT-HAND PAGE
Treated like fresh-cut
flowers, with their stalks
in water, artichokes will
stay fresh longer.

ABOVE
Pink-veined coco
rose beans are
essential for making
a pistou soup.

Carrots

In the past, to preserve carrots in the winter months the carrots were placed at the bottom of a box or stoneware pot and then covered with thick layers of sand to keep them cool.

∾ Warning: once cooked, carrots should be consumed on the same day as they oxidize very quickly and then become unfit for consumption (this applies especially to young children).

Basil sauce

1 BUNCH OF REALLY FRESH BASIL

2 CRUSHED GARLIC CLOVES

100G (4OZ) GRATED PARMESAN

½ GLASS FRUITY OLIVE OIL

SALT AND PEPPER

1. Remove the stalks from the basil, and keep only the tender leaves.
2. Place them in a food processor. Add the crushed garlic, oil and grated Parmesan.
3. Mix to obtain a creamy, pale-green sauce. Add pepper and salt.

This sauce is ideal for use with fresh pasta, noodles or alternatively in a pesto soup. Once you have taken the quantity you need, then add some more oil to the mixture.

∾ In order to prevent raw carrots oxidizing and turning an ugly brown color once they are chopped, just toss the prepared vegetables in some lemon juice.

Herbs

∾ To prolong their lifespan, roll the herbs in a damp cloth and keep in the fridge.

∾ Delicate herbs, such as fresh coriander or basil, can be kept in a closed glass jar.

∾ To chop herbs more easily, snip and cut them with scissors in a glass or glass bowl until you end up with a fine mixture.

∾ You can use herb ice cubes to flavor a stew or soup. This is done by putting finely chopped herbs in an ice-cube tray and then covering with water.

∾ Parsley can be both curly or flat-leaved. The flat-leaved variety is preferable to curly-leaved as it has more flavor. However, curly-leaved parsley can be prepared in an original way by dipping it in hot fat for a few seconds. Enhanced in this fashion, it will provide the perfect garnish for fish or roast meat.

Perserved herbs

In the past, so as to be able to use herbs in the middle of winter, housewives used to preserve them in salt.

∾ To preserve herbs in this way, alternate a layer of herbs (parsley, chives, tarragon or any other herb of your choice, in sufficient quantity to fill the receptacle) with a layer of coarse salt in a tightly closed stoneware jar. You can then take out the necessary quantity whenever you want to flavor a soup or a stew.

Garlic

❧ To make the most of the flavor of garlic, without suffering from digestive problems, simply rub the cooking dish with a raw garlic clove: this is a process that is often used to flavor a *gratin dauphinois*.

❧ To stuff a leg of lamb or roast beef with garlic, cut the cloves into thin spikes and push them in horizontally, not vertically.

❧ Unlike onion sprouts, garlic sprouts should be removed because they make garlic hard to digest. To serve a garlic cream with roast meat, cook a dozen unpeeled garlic cloves until golden. When they are tender, simply scrape out the pulp.

Onion

Onions are best kept in an airy place away from sunlight and humidity.

❧ If onions sprout, do not throw away the green stalks as they can be used in salads or other dishes. You will be positively glad of sprouting onions in winter, when chives are rare and expensive. In order to make an onion sprout, put one atop a flared-neck jug, filled with water. In less than ten days you will have many fresh and delicious green sprouts.

ABOVE
Garlic can be purchased
in garlands or singly, and
is an essential ingredient
in the kitchen – health giving
as well as delicious.

RIGHT-HAND PAGE
This ordinary onion nests
in a hyacinth vase. In a few
days it will sprout green stalks
that taste just like chives
and can be used in salads.

Eugénie's garlic tourin

Discovered in the recipe book that belonged to a great-grandmother from Normandy, this recipe derives originally from Béarn and can be prepared equally well with garlic or onion. It is the inclusion of the egg mixture that makes this dish so special.

15ML (1TBSP) OLIVE OIL

5 GARLIC CLOVES, FINELY CHOPPED

15ML (1TBSP) PLAIN FLOUR

1L (1¾PT) WATER

1 EGG, SEPARATED

15ML (1TBSP) CRÈME FRÂICHE

ENOUGH SLICES OF TOASTED BREAD

FOR THE NUMBER OF GUESTS

SALT AND PEPPER

1. Gently heat the olive oil in a pan and then cook the chopped garlic cloves until they are golden.

2. When golden, add the flour to the chopped garlic and let it brown slightly.

3. Pour in the boiling water, add the lightly beaten egg white and season.

4. Cook the mixture for 10 minutes. This is what is called the tourin.

5. At the bottom of a soup tureen beat the egg yolk and mix in the crème fraîche.

6. Pour the boiling tourin into the tureen.

7. Lay one slice of toast in each soup bowl and serve immediately.

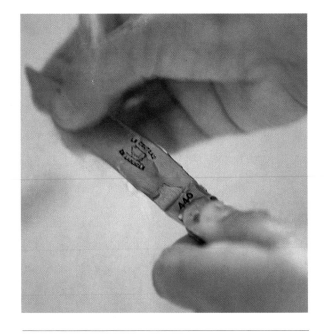

Tip

To eradicate the smell of raw garlic or onion from your fingers, there is a very simple trick – slide your fingers carefully along the blade of a stainless-steel knife, under running water. Instant success guaranteed!

Fish

When purchasing fish, ensure that they are firm, with shiny scales and eyes intact even when on the fishmonger's stall. The surest sign of a healthy fish is that the gills are bright red.

In Turkish markets, fishermen turn the gills of the fish inside out so that the buyer can see how fresh their fish is. This makes the fish appear strangely decorated with fantastic red eyelets...

To bone your fish, use tweezers or fine pincers.

To scale fish easily, you can make a practical tool by nailing several lines of metallic bottlecaps on to a flat piece of wood: the teeth of the caps will scale the fish well.

Food preservation

Before the invention of fridges and freezers, preserving fresh food was a major preoccupation. Vegetables were pickled in brine for a few hours after picking and, when not candied or preserved in alcohol, fruits were dried. Fruits such as apples, pears, grapes, figs and tomatoes were dried in farm cellars. Meat and dried meats were salted, smoked – many country houses had their own smoking oven – or preserved in fat. These supplies, often laid down during summer, made it possible to have a variety of different foods throughout the winter months, compensating for the lack of fresh produce during that season.

The fruit storeroom

The best temperature to preserve your fruit in a fruit storeroom is around 4–5°C (39–41°F).

Old books on household management recommend choosing a dark room with as little air as possible and ideally facing towards the east.

Apples and pears

When storing these fruits in a fruit storeroom or on a shelf, place the apples standing up but the pears stalk down.

A drop of wax at the end of the stalk will help the fruit last longer.

Figs

Black or green figs are at their tastiest when they seem to be weeping and are covered with juice.

If you live in a sunny and warm region and are lucky enough to have a fig tree, you can dry figs. Pick the figs during the autumn, then dry them by spreading them on racks outside.

Flattened apples and pears

1KG (2¼LB) APPLES

1KG (2¼LB) PEARS

1. Peel the apples and pears, halve them and remove the cores.
2. Spread the peeled fruits on the oven shelf and then set the oven to a minimum temperature: Leave them to dry in the oven for at least 4 hours.
3. Once dry, the fruits are flattened with the back of a wooden spoon, hence their name.

LEFT-HAND PAGE
Pears will keep longer in the coolness of an old-fashioned fruit storeroom when they have a drop of wax on their stalks.

OVERLEAF
Bay leaves impart their distinctive flavor to drying figs. The best dried figs are recognized by the familiar sugar-like white powder that mists them with a soft bloom.

∽ Once they have been dried, figs will keep for a very long time. They will acquire a delicious flavor if packed with bay or peach leaves (to do this, alternate a layer of fruit with a layer of leaves) in a wooden box.

∽ Bay leaves can also be used to flavor raisins. Just sprinkle the raisins with sugar then store in a wooden box, in the same way as the figs.

Tomatoes

Italians often dry tomatoes in the loft, but they can be dried just as well in the oven, at its lowest setting.

Walnuts

In the olden days, walnuts were put in large jars filled with sand, so that they would stay fresh longer.

∽ If you would like to get the taste of fresh walnuts from dried ones, soak them for several hours in fresh milk before use.

Grapes

In the past, grapes were eaten right up to Christmas. They were preserved from the cold (but also heat) and humidity, to keep them in good condition.

∽ In an old-fashioned preserving process, grapes were placed stalk first in a bottle or pitcher filled with water. Used in the past in Thomery, near Fontainebleau in the Parisian area, a small town renowned for its white Chasselas grape, this preserving method is still practised in the fruit storeroom of the Domain of Saint-Jean-De-

Oven-dried tomatoes

1KG (2¼LB) RIPE

AND FLAVORSOME TOMATOES

COARSE SALT

OLIVE OIL

1. Cut the tomatoes horizontally in half, sprinkle with coarse salt (or a very fine and highly prized French salt, fleur de sel) and lay them cut-side down on a greased baking sheet.

2. Place them in the oven at 120°C (250°F/Gas mark ½) for at least 4 hours. The flesh must still be springy, but not juicy.

3. Put them in a jar and fill it with a good-quality fruity olive oil.

Tip

*To make decorations with your fruits or flowers
(for a festive table, for example), roll them in very sweet
water, then in sugar, and then leave to dry.
Another more refined method consists of brushing
the fruit or flowers, such as roses or violets, with
a whisked egg white. Roll them next in sifted icing
sugar, and you will have fruits or flowers that
look frosted once dried.*

BELOW
*In an old-fashioned preserving
method, grapes were balanced
stalk-down in a bottle or
pitcher that was filled
with water.*

Beauregard, where, incidentally, it is possible to admire one of the most beautiful vegetable gardens and orchards in Europe.

∼ Alternatively, one can hang grapes with a thread, simply secured to their stalk. This used to be done in the South of France and in Italy, where the grapes were kept in a light and airy room.

Candied fruit and jams

Candied fruit and jams appeared in France quite late in history, as sugar was considered to be a luxury. Catherine de Medici introduced sweets at court in the sixteenth century. One of the first to devise genuine recipes for candied fruit and jams, still usable today if adapted, was a gentleman from St-Rémy-de-Provence, Michel de Notre-Dame, better known as Nostradamus who wrote *The Prophesies*, a collection of predictions for the years to come.

Candied fruit

The preparation of candied fruit is time consuming, and several steps are necessary.

∼ Prick the skin of the fruit. Blanch for a few minutes in boiling water then soak in cold water overnight. Cook again in water for a very short time, then dip in cool water before draining. Finally, cook the fruit in sugar syrup until they look translucid. Spread out on greaseproof paper to dry.

∼ Some old recipe books advise adding a pinch of alum (bought from a chemists) to the water used to blanch the fruit, when they are slightly overripe or a little soft. This will make them firmer.

Jam

⤳ To check when a jam is set, dip a spoon in the boiling liquid and place a few drops on a cold plate. If the jam runs in a thick syrup, cook it for a little longer. But if it forms thick drops and does not run, stop cooking immediately.

⤳ To set jams without using pectin sugar, add an apple core with its pips and the peel secured in a small cloth bag to the preparation. Naturally rich in pectin, these will help the jam to set.

⤳ Give your apricot, plum or cherry jam an almond flavor by cooking a few crushed fruit stones, enclosed in a small muslin bag, at the same time as the fruits.

⤳ The jam must be poured into sterilized jars the instant it is ready. Leave for 48 hours before sealing the pots, so that the jam can fully set. Cut rounds of greaseproof paper the size of the pots and dip them in brandy before laying them on top of the jam. Then cover the pots with a square of white or brown parcel wrap and tie with string or a small linen ribbon. For a final touch, stick on a label with the name of the fruit and the year.

⤳ If a jam goes mouldy, it means that it was not cooked for long enough. Remove all traces of mould and cook again.

⤳ Similarly, a jam that has been overcooked and has crystallized can be salvaged by cooking it again with the juice of a lemon.

⤳ To obtain a lovely soft fruit jelly, use a special dish towel made of cotton muslin, similar to a thickly woofed gauze, as a filter. You could also use a large square of butter muslin.

LEFT-HAND PAGE
A true old-fashioned orange
marmalade is made with
a combination of sweet and
bitter oranges, found in winter.

Lila's bitter orange marmalade

FOR ABOUT 30 POTS
12 BITTER ORANGES
6 SWEET ORANGES
4 LEMONS
8KG (17LB) GRANULATED SUGAR
12L (2¾GAL) WATER

1. Slice the whole fruits, unpeeled, very thinly. Set the pips aside, in a bowl with a little water.
2. Place the fruit slices in a large china or enamel bowl and cover with water. Leave to soak overnight.
3. The following day, pour the water and fruit into a preserving pan and cook for 2 hours.
4. Take the pan off the heat, add the sugar and leave again overnight.
5. The following day, filter the water containing the pips; they will have formed a jelly that you add to the preserving pan. Simmer for over an hour, until the marmalade sets.

Having lived some years in Morocco, Lila used to make her marmalade with bigarade oranges, whose sweet-and-sour flesh was perfect for marmalade making. They can only be found in France in Provence, or when ordered from certain greengrocers.

She used to prepare her reserve of orange marmalade in winter, hence the quantities to last a year, but you can reduce them if you wish.

33

Eugénie's Normandy fat

450G (1LB) BEEF KIDNEY FAT

(ORDER IN ADVANCE FROM

YOUR BUTCHER)

150G (5OZ) LEEKS

150G (5OZ) ONIONS

150G (5OZ) TURNIPS

1 CELERY STICK

1 PARSLEY SPRIG

2 SPRIGS THYME

1 GARLIC BULB

SALT AND PEPPER

1. Cut the cold fat into chunky cubes and melt it gently in a heavy-based pan or a cast-iron pot. While it is melting, slice all the vegetables.

2. Add the vegetables to the fat with the herbs and garlic. Stir. Season with salt and pepper to taste.

3. Pour the fat, still hot, into a glass jar or a stoneware pot, seal tightly and then store in a cool place.

This fat keeps for a long time and can be used in soups and stews, giving them a unique flavor.

Vegetable preserves

∾ Make a point of always boiling your preserving pots before filling them with the vegetables to be sterilized or pickled.

∾ In order that glass pots do not bang together in the steam cooker during the boiling process, wrap them in a dish towel or thin cloth.

∾ If you want to preserve tomatoes, use firm fruits. Plum or Roma tomatoes are ideal for this, as long as they are not overripe.

∾ For extra flavor add pepper, herbs (tarragon, basil, celery, flat-leaved parsley, dill) and spices (coriander seeds, cloves, cardamom, chillies) to vegetables.

∾ Do not wash gherkins. Simply scatter a layer of coarse salt on a clean tea towel, enclose the gherkins in the cloth, then rub vigorously.

∾ The gherkins will be crunchier if you add a sugar cube to the preserving vinegar.

RIGHT-HAND PAGE
An appetizing window,
where preserving pots
are cooled before being
stored away in a dark
larder or storeroom.

Butter, eggs, cheese and milk

⤳ Cows and chickens are essential farm livestock. Wonderfully fresh cows' milk means that cream, butter and cheese can be prepared at home, and there is nothing to beat a newly laid egg for flavor. With the help of household-management books and cookbooks, housewives learned how to preserve cheese and butter, which otherwise tended to go rancid quickly, as well as how to recognize how fresh eggs were. ⤳

Ensuring eggs are fresh

⤳ Nowadays eggs are dated, but there is a traditional way to identify truly fresh eggs. To enjoy them soft-boiled, immerse them in a container filled with 15 percent salted water (150g/6oz coarse salt for 1/1¾pt water). Fresh eggs will sink. If they are more than five days old, they contain more air and will float back up to the surface. If they do this, you are best advised to throw them away.

⤳ When fridges did not exist, eggs were usually kept wrapped in several sheets of newspaper. Sometimes they were buried under ashes, woodchips or sand. Another way to preserve them is to brush the shell with oil, lard or petroleum jelly.

Cooking eggs

⤳ To prevent eggs from bursting during cooking, prick each end with a thick needle and add a spoonful of vinegar to the cooking water.

⤳ To prepare perfect soft-boiled eggs, place them in a large bowl, pour a saucepan of boiling water over, then cover and wait seven minutes before tucking in.

⤳ Children love dipping thickly buttered "soldiers" in the yolk of a soft-boiled egg. As an alternative, bread can be replaced by warm asparagus or cooked cheese sticks or even olive or anchovy focaccia.

⤳ To distinguish a raw from a cooked egg, spin it. A raw egg turns with difficulty, while a cooked egg turns like a spinning top.

Old-fashioned fried eggs

1 LARGE CUBE OF BUTTER

2 EGGS, SEPARATED

SALT AND PEPPER

Never sprinkle salt over the egg yolk when frying an egg because white specks will form and spoil the appearance.

1. In a small round flameproof china dish, melt the butter and add a little salt and pepper. When the butter starts to turn golden, pour the egg whites in and cook.

2. When the white is set, add the yolks and cook for a further few seconds.

Preserving butter

⤳ To keep butter for longer, wrap it in a cloth dipped in vinegar or lemon water (just a few drops of either of these is enough).

⤳ In hot weather, if you do not want to keep butter in the fridge, where it may become too hard, place it on a plate and cover it with an earthenware pot that has been dipped in water. Wet the pot every day. The butter will keep and stay fresh through the evaporation of the water from the clay.

⤳ To present butter in an attractive way, wrap it in a fresh cabbage or sorrel leaf (but not for too long, so the taste of the leaf is not transferred to the butter).

Refreshening rancid butter

15ML (3TBSP) BICARBONATE OF SODA

150G (5OZ) BUTTER

1 BAY LEAF

SALTED WATER

1. Stir the bicarbonate of soda into a large bowl of iced water, then work the butter in thoroughly. The bicarbonate destroys the germs responsible for fermentation and neutralizes the rancid taste of the butter.

2. Place the bay leaf in the base of a clean container and add the butter. Pour salted water over to cover. Bay oil, an antiseptic, helps to preserve the butter for longer.

Preserving butter with salt

If you buy butter in slabs, this is an easy way to preserve it and prevents it from turning rancid to quickly.

REQUIRED QUANTITY OF BUTTER

TO FILL A POT OR JAR

115G (4OZ) SALT

1L (1¾PT) WATER

1. Prepare a 10 per cent salt solution: bring the water to the boil and add the salt as soon as it starts boiling. Leave to boil for just a few seconds then remove from the heat.

2. When the water has cooled completely, pour it over the butter in a stoneware or glass jar or pot. Store in a cool place.

Alexandre Dumas' butter recipe

In his *Grand Dictionnaire de Cuisine*, Alexandre Dumas advocates an astonishing method: "Whatever country I found myself in, I always had fresh butter made that very day. I give my recipe to travellers; it is quite simple and at the same time infallible. Wherever I could get milk, from cows, camels, mares or especially sheep, I would fill three-quarters of a bottle, close it, hang it around my horse's neck and then let my horse do the rest. In the evening, I would break the neck of the bottle and find that a clump of butter, the size of a fist, had formed of its own accord... This method has never failed me."

Preserving cheese

∿ Place cheeses under a cheese-bell and put a few sugar cubes on the platter: the cubes will absorb the excess moisture.

∿ Wrap hard cheeses in a cloth previously dipped in white wine and then wrung out.

Milk

When milk was neither pasteurized nor sterilized nor homogenized, it had to be boiled before consumption. As it was whole, a thick layer of cream formed at the top. This was carefully skimmed off by housewives, who would use it in cake making or cooking.

∿ Rinse a saucepan quickly with cold water before pouring in milk, to prevent it from sticking.

∿ To stop the milk from overflowing during heating, simply put a metal teaspoon or a saucer at the bottom of the pan.

∿ Improve the peculiar taste of powdered milk by adding a little salt to the water.

Making curdled milk or yogurt

Curdled milk, highly appreciated in the past, was replaced by the yogurt that we eat today. By straining curdled milk through a muslin cloth, it loses its whey and becomes like fromage frais, to which you can add herbs and pepper. Alternatively, you can sweeten it with honey, jam or brown sugar.

LEFT-HAND PAGE
Cheeses under a cheese-bell.
They keep better if
you place a few sugar
cubes on the platter and
let a little air circulate
(use a sugar cube to keep the
bell slightly jacked up).

Home-made cheese

CHEESE LEFTOVERS

ALL OF SIMILAR TYPE AND FLAVOR

HALF THEIR WEIGHT IN BUTTER OR

CRÈME FRÂICHE

BREADCRUMBS OR FINELY

CHOPPED HERBS

1. Remove the rind from the cheese leftovers.
2. Then mix the cheese leftover pieces in a food processor with the butter or crème fraîche until the mixture is smooth.
3. Wet the palm of your hands and shape the paste into balls, then roll them, one at a time, in breadcrumbs or herbs.

Roquefort with port

175G (6OZ) ROQUEFORT

75G (3OZ) BUTTER, SOFTENED

15ML (1TBSP) PORT

1. Work the Roquefort and softened butter together with a fork until you obtain a smooth, creamy and thick paste.
2. Add the port to the thick cheese paste and mix it thoroughly.
3. Pour this preparation into an attractive glass cup or a stoneware pot and keep in the fridge. Remember to take it out of the fridge at least 1 hour before serving.

To encourage it to turn more quickly into curdled milk, add an artichoke in a small muslin cloth bag to the raw milk, and place in a warm room.

In Provence country housewives rubbed the inside of a tureen with wild thyme or mother-of-thyme: this was enough to make the milk curdle.

By mixing a pot of yogurt with fresh raw milk in a cup and leaving it in a warm place overnight, you will get a jar of delicious yogurt.

Grandma's real café au lait*

1 BOWL OF SWEETENED CAFÉ AU LAIT

2 SLICES OF BUTTERED BREAD

A PINCH OF SALT

1. Pour the sweetened café au lait into an oven proof china bowl.

2. Place the buttered bread slices on the surface of the coffee.

3. Place the bowl in a hot oven and bake until the surface of the mixture has become a crunchy, melting crust.

Colette, the French writer, gave the recipe of this "caretaker's café au lait" in Chéri *and in the magazine* Marie-Claire *in 1939. Last advice from the writer: "Before breaking into your bread raft, sprinkle it with salt. The salt gives the sugar bite; slightly salted sugar is yet another important principle neglected in many Parisian puddings and pastries, which become bland and tasteless."*
(Colette Gourmande, *Marie-Christine and Didier* Clément, *Albin Michel, 1990.)*

Milk jam with the sweetness of childhood

Those who still remember the taste of sweet condensed milk, eaten straight out of the tin, will love the caramelized sweetness of milk jam. This pudding is probably Argentinian in origin: in Argentina it is called *dulce de leche*, literally *milk sweet.*

This jam is very simple to make. Simply cook an unopened tin of sweetened condensed milk in a bain-marie for an hour and a half (or two if you prefer a thicker consistency). Leave it to cool before opening the tin and savor the *dulce*, a pure treat for children and adults alike.

Curdled milk or yogurt with dried fruit and honey

1 GLASS DRIED APRICOTS, RAISINS AND

PRUNES, STONED

1 LARGE BOWL OF DRAINED CURDLED MILK

OR YOGURT

30ML (2TBSP) CLEAR HONEY

GRATED PEEL OF ½ AN UNTREATED ORANGE

1. Cut the dried fruit into thin slices and soak for a few minutes in boiling water so that they swell. Drain any excess liquid.

2. Mix the soaked fruit into the curdled milk or yogurt.

3. Add the honey and grated peel. Chill for at least 1 hour before serving.

Cake-making hints and tips

∾ *Pastry and cake making can be so easy as long as certain tricks associated with elementary chemistry are used. Practice is still the best way and cooks learn to master these techniques by tackling numerous different recipes. With experience, pastry-makers have learnt to leave pie pastry in a cool place before cooking it. On the other hand, soufflés must be baked in the oven immediately after preparation. Cooks also learn to knead pastry quickly and lightly with cool hands (if necessary, by dipping them first in cold water), as they know that a pastry that has been kneaded too long will become unpalatably hard after cooking.* ∾

Tarts

Whether it be shortcrust, flaky or puff, pastry must be left for a while before being cooked in the oven, so that butter and flour combine fully.

∾ Never knead pastry too long, or it will harden during cooking.

∾ So that halved plums, peaches and apricots do not soak the pastry, position them rounded-side, not cut side, on the pastry.

∾ A fine layer of breadcrumbs or egg white brushed on to the pastry will absorb excess juices.

Dried and candied fruit

∾ To prevent dried or candied fruit from sinking to the bottom of a cake, roll them in flour before adding them to the liquid mixture. The simplest way to do this is to put them in a small polythene bag (a freezer bag, for example) with some flour. Close the bag and then shake vigorously.

∾ Before using them in the mixture for a compote or for a cake, soak prunes and dried apricots in a strong tea infusion, which will endow them with a much greater depth of flavor.

Instant shortcrust pastry

150G (5OZ) BUTTER

½ GLASS OF WATER

A PINCH OF SALT

275G (10OZ) PLAIN FLOUR

FOR SWEET PASTRY: 115G (4OZ)

GRANULATED SUGAR

1. Melt the butter over a very low heat. When liquid, take off the heat and add the water and salt. Pour in the flour in one go. Add the sugar, if using. Mix with a wooden spoon until a ball of dough is formed.

2. Grease a tart dish. Spread out the pastry uniformly, while still warm, with the back of the hand, ensuring an even thickness.

3. Prick the bottom of the pastry with a fork and then trace diagonal lines all around the edge to flatten it.

A quicker way to caramelize

∿ Use a small blowtorch to caramelize the top of a crème brûlée or any other pudding requiring a thin layer of caramel. It is faster than the oven, grill or the round iron used by Catalan cooks for their famous crème brûlée.

Golden cakes

∿ Simply brush uncooked cake mixture when in the tin with egg yolk to make it come out golden and shiny. If you do not have any egg yolk, fresh milk is always a perfect substitute.

∿ While your cakes are baking, especially meringues, (and indeed soufflés or any preparation containing whisked egg whites), it is crucial to remember to keep the oven door closed at all times, otherwise the cake mixture inside will deflate and the result will be as flat as a pancake.

Flavored sugar

∿ A few vanilla pods cut in half and placed in a bowl of granulated or castor sugar will give it an inimitable flavor.

∿ To make an unusual flavored sugar, alternate a layer of dried lavender with a layer of sugar in a sugar bowl. This lavender sugar can be used within fruit salads, creams or cakes.

Jean's plume cake

Jean was a writer, a grandfather and an enthusiastic pudding maker. The name of his recipe is a play on words, alluding to both his work (plume meaning pen) and the English plum cake, full of raisins and currants, on which it is based.

225G (8OZ) MIXED RAISINS
AND CURRANTS

1 SHERRY GLASS OF RUM

175G (6OZ) BUTTER

A PINCH OF SALT

4 EGGS

½ SACHET OF YEAST

175G (6OZ) GRANULATED SUGAR

250G (9OZ) PLAIN FLOUR

CHOPPED PEEL OF ½ A LEMON

1. Soak the raisins and currants in the rum.

2. Cut the butter, softened at room temperature, into small cubes in a large terrine dish.

3. Add the sugar and salt and whisk thoroughly until the mixture becomes pale.

4. Whisk the eggs in thoroughly, one at a time.

5. Add the yeast to the flour and sprinkle the flour into the dish.

6. Mix the mixture with a wooden spoon, lifting it to introduce air and make it lighter.

7. Drain the dried fruit. Coat them in flour and incorporate into the mixture with the chopped lemon peel.

8. Grease a bread tin and preheat the oven to 180°C (350°F/ Gas mark 4). Pour the mixture into the tin and put in the oven.

9. Cook for 10 minutes, then lower the heat to 140°C (275°F/ Gas mark 1). Cook for a further 50 minutes. The cake is cooked when a knife blade inserted into the mixture comes out dry. If the top of the cake browns too much towards the end of its cooking time, cover it with foil.

HOME
sweet home

"*I* will describe her life and her home to you as I remember it: the rooms where life was lived; the bedrooms drenched with sunlight in the morning; the floor festooned with apricot, red and ochre Oriental rugs inherited from her mother-in-law, which seemed to absorb the light and retain the heat despite their age. There were books, dried flowers and cushions inspired by the colors of Matisse; and objects sparkling with an authenticity that, had they been owned by an ancient community, would have been placed in graves for the next life: crystal dice, bits of stag antlers, amber pearls, boxes, sculptures, wooden balls..."
James Salter, *Un Bonheur Parfait* (*Perfect Happiness*), published by Editions de l'Olivier, 1997.

A house often shares characteristics with its owners, who have furnished it and decorated it with eclectic objects collected haphazardly over the years, with no regard for fashion or custom; this results in a sense of comfort and a palable feeling of the rhythms of life within its four walls. Improvised curtains; lit candles; sylvan, fruity or spicy perfumes; flowers changed every week, bright or light paint can be enough to give it new life without changing too much of its indefinable charm. From generation to generation, practical hints are handed down that are as useful today as they were in previous ages, allowing us to rediscover the pleasure of making, embellishing and cooking without hurrying: taking time simply to live...

Patience is acquired and imagination too. All you need to do is to look, feel and touch each thing in a new way, so that daily life becomes a continuous celebration.

Traditional paints

❧ *Colors such as those seen on old walls and in lived-in houses tell a story. Yellows, reds and ochres are connected with the South of France, whereas light tones of grey, beige and blue are more often linked with the North.*

The eye can also be captivated by emerald green or the unusual red of an Irish or Scandinavian door...or that distinctive blue used in Greece, Morocco, Turkey and the Orient, which in France is called "cart blue" or "cartwright blue". First made from mixing methylene blue with lime, this unmistakable colour was used by farmers to paint doors, windows, harnesses and carts, as it was supposed to keep flies at bay... ❧

Milk paint

Milk is often used as a binder for ground pigments. The result is a paint that colors wood and plaster easily (it is the principle of casein paints, often used in olden days). Once dry, it is translucid and shiny, unless you add lime for a thicker consistency.

❧ Milk paint is still used today for restoring old houses as well as old painted panelling and furniture. The surface must be matt and sanded before painting; Protect the paint with varnish, particularly if using outdoors, as it is fairly fragile.

❧ Pigment-based paints have been used since prehistoric times. To get the coloured powders to adhere to walls, different bases have been used, in particular milk and casein, egg, or animal glues (fish or rabbit), which are still sold today in shops that specialize in materials for craftmen and painters.

Milk paint

1 PACKET OF POWDERED PIGMENT
(THE QUANTITY USED WILL DEPEND ON
THE RESULT WANTED, WHETHER DARKER
OR LIGHTER)
1L (1¾PT) MILK

1. Gradually dilute the pigment in the milk, until a fairly thick creamy consistency is obtained.
2. Add more pigment if you find the tone too light for your requirements.

LEFT-HAND PAGE
In a bedroom of the Château de Giniac, antique cushions harmonize with a wall painted traditionally with lime and a blue pigment, topped with a scalloped edge.

~ Pigments make it possible to invent all sorts of shades and to achieve sheens totally different from those obtained with the acrylic or solvent-based paints that are generally used today.

ABOVE
Blue is traditionally the color of the coat of the Virgin Mary, depicted in church statues wearing the color of a clear blue summer sky.

RIGHT-HAND PAGE
Ground pigments must be diluted in a liquid: milk, animal glue or egg, for example, so they will attach to the surface to be painted.

Lime paint

4L (7PT) WATER

2KG (4½LB) LIME

700G (1LB 10OZ) COARSE SALT

1 PACKET OF POWDERED PIGMENT

1. Pour the lime into the water, stir thoroughly, and leave overnight.

2. The following day, add the salt dissolved in 2l (3½pt) boiling water. Stir thoroughly then add as much pigment as necessary, until you achieve the desired color.

This paint, much used in the past, enables you to freshen up your house from top to bottom every year. Be careful though, as the color always seems darker before drying. Test it first to see what it will eventually look like.

Tips

Try this old method to absorb the smell of oil-based or solvent-based paint: place several saucers of fresh milk or hot vinegar in the room. To avoid any paint stains on a mirror or window, rub the cut side of an onion across the entire surface of the glass: this will stop the paint from sticking to it.

Light

"A lamp behind the window keeps watch in the secret heart of the night."
Antée, C. Barucoa, *in* La Flamme d'une Chandelle, *Gaston Bachelard, Puf, 1962.*

∾ *Whether from a lamp, lantern, fire or candle, light steals away the threatening cloak of darkness. From the outside a light has a reassuring effect, telling the passer-by that the house is alive and inhabited.*

There is no need to flood the house with light; it is more interesting to play with different sources of light and variations of brightness. Traditional bulbs emit a warm yellow glow, while candles confer a magical ambience on even the humblest place.

You can also adorn the night with lanterns that capture flames within their glass walls, placing them on windowsills, along a path or in a tree in the garden...∾

Windows adorned with charm and simplicity

∾ If you like simplicity and natural style, you can dress your windows with white or colored linen or cotton drapes. In flea markets, for example, you can still find thick linen or white and ecru hemp drapes, which are perfect for a charmingly naive decor.

∾ An old drape, embellished with embroidery, lace or a monogram, will filter the sunlight. You can have the adornment at the top by folding back a few inches of the material, like a hanging flounce, or, if you have a monogram or embroidered edge, leave it at the bottom, for an elegant hem.

∾ With a fairly narrow window, use Scandinavian curtains as inspiration. These are made of a light net curtain, flat-mounted and pulled up on only one side of the window by a tie or an eyelet hung to a brass tack or polished metal nail.

Lila's stained-glass curtain

2 LINEN OR LINEN-COTTON WHITE DRAPES

PIECES OF PRETTY COLORED GLASS,

COLLECTED AT THE SEASIDE

EMBROIDERY THREAD

1. Place the pieces of glass between the two sheets and sew around the edges with a slanting stitch to secure the glass in place.

2. With very sharp scissors, cut a small hole, either narrow, large, round or elongated, to match the pebbles' shapes.

3. Embroider the edges of these holes using a buttonhole stitch.

Inspired by embroidered cloths from regions of western India such as Rajasthan, Sind or Gujarat, Lila, more than 30 years ago, imitated young Indian brides who would bring in their trousseau, as part of their dowry, cloths, drapes or animal harnesses that had often been embellished with tiny pearls or glass splinters stitched into the fabric. This project is a time consuming one (it took about a year to make this curtain!) but the finished result is well worth it.

Once finished, this curtain is rather heavy and will need to be washed by hand (in a machine the glass fragments will break up and spoil the material). You could use shells, or other decorative attachments, instead of these shiny adornments if preferred.

~ To freshen up a room in summer, during very hot weather, dampen the whole curtain using a water spray and leave the windows open. By passing through the damp fabric, the air will have a fresher quality.

Curtains from far away

Soft or bright-colored cotton saris can be used to make precious-looking curtains or even drapes over a four-poster bed or bay window. A sari is sufficient to adorn a double window or a four-poster bed with billowing folds falling around the sides. You can find saris at exhibitions on Indian culture, costume or crafts or in specialist Indian sari shops.

ABOVE
Tiny mirrors and glass
pebbles are set in cotton
with embroidery stitches.

RIGHT-HAND PAGE
This stained-glass curtain
will stay forever unfinished,
as its creator intended.

Original tie-backs

To enhance a curtain, you can use other things than traditional curtain fitments.

∾ You might like to tie shells to a thick rope made of rough string.

∾ A multi-colored scarf, a necklace made of big colored pearls or shells, or even a bracelet (for a net curtain) can make a fetching tie-back.

∾ For a special occasion, you can buy raffia ropes in a garden centre and add fresh leaves or the leaves of artificial flowers to it (but fresh flowers will last only the length of an "alfresco dinner").

Half curtains

The term "half-curtain,"–"*brise-bise*" (wind-cutter) in French – is a relatively recent coinage that seems to have appeared only at the end of the nineteenth century. This suggests that these short curtains, hung at the bottom half of the window to stop cold draughts, were not used before that time.

∾ A finely striped dish towel, a damask tablecloth or even a large traditional handkerchief with white and blue or white and red checks can be made into lovely half- curtains for a kitchen or bathroom. You will need as many half-curtains as window panes, thin metal-curtain rails or bamboo stakes (ideal in a countryside or seaside house) and clipping rings (about five or six per pane). All you have to do is clip the rings to the fabric at regular intervals and then slide them on to the rail.

Tip

Butter muslin, which is very thin and light, can replace a traditional net curtain perfectly. However, it does become crinkled after washing. You can keep these pleats, which give them the appearance of the Spanish designer Fortuny's fabrics. Or you can iron them out when the muslin is still damp.

LEFT
A temporary tie-back, made with flowers and leaves attached to a raffia rope, is a delightful touch for a special occasion.

RIGHT-HAND PAGE
Lovely cotton damask napkins, embroidered with an ancient monogram, have been turned into kitchen half-curtains. See without being seen...

Making your own candles

1. Collect the remaining wax of melted candle stumps and heat them in a bain-marie to melt them again.

2. Pour this wax into heatproof glass or pretty oiled moulds, perfumed with a few drops of essential oil or incense.

3. You will find candle wicks in craft shops and some large DIY stores. To ensure that they stay straight in the liquid wax, tie the wicks to a pen that is placed across the receptacle into which you have poured the wax.

Candles

Candle wax is a delicate material, which scratches and breaks easily. If you like to keep a good stock of different colored candles, wrap them in colorless silk paper (colored paper could stain the wax).

∽ If you want to restore shine to your candles when they have become dusty or are slightly damaged, slip an old stocking on your hand and gently rub the surface to polish them.

∽ To fit a candle in a chandelier whose openings are narrow, simply soften the wax by dipping the candle in hot water for a few seconds.

∽ Keep your candles away from any source of heat: even the sun can soften them and cause them to become contorted.

∽ Candle stains are easy to erase, as long as the wax is colorless. Scrape off as much as you can using a knife blade. Then place a piece of silk or kitchen paper over the stain and iron with a hot iron. Repeat with fresh fabric or paper until no wax remains. Then wash the fabric as usual.

∽ To prevent a new candle from dripping, light it, leave it to burn for a few seconds, then pour a thick layer of fine salt around the wick. You can also dip your candles in highly salted water or leave them overnight in the freezer.

ABOVE
Lovers of candlelight always have plentiful provisions so that they can create a magical atmosphere whenever the mood takes them.

RIGHT-HAND PAGE
Ingenious glass baubles on a decorative candelabra catch drips of wax and prevent fabric and furniture underneath from becoming stained.

The art of the wood fire

To light a fire easily, certain rules must be followed.
❧ "Always have, as well as burning wood, very dry firewood, which not only makes it easier to start the fire, but also gives it a very jolly 'sparkly' aspect, called *flambées*, emanating heat and gaiety into the room," advised the Countess of Gence in her *Encyclopédie de La Vie Pratique* (*Encyclopaedia of Practical Life*).

❧ You can also use pine cones collected from the forest (they are pleasant to look at, burn quickly and emit a marvellous scent), newspaper or very dry logs. Chopped wood must dry for a year before being burned; if too green, it burns badly and gives out more smoke than heat.

❧ Make a pyramid in the hearth, the base of newspaper and small pieces of wood. When they start burning, add the logs, letting air circulate between them to fan the flames.

Choosing wood

In town it is impossible to choose your wood, but in the countryside it can be useful to find various sorts of wood, as recommended in old home-economic books. One of these advises that "A good fire must be made with different types of wood. Oak lasts longer than beech. A fire made of oak, beech and elm will be perfect, as these last two types will give a lot of embers." Of all the woods, walnut gives out the most heat, followed by the pear tree, oak, chestnut and ash.

❧ If you live near the sea collect flotsam wood from the shore. It makes very good lighting fuel and often emits a marvellous scent (perhaps because it is imbued with sea salt).

❧ If you live in a wine-growing area, collect grape shoots, which are ideal for a blazing fire. They are also excellent for barbecues as they will give a lovely flavor to grilled food.

❧ Be careful of wood that spits: splinters from pine wood can create a fire hazard if you do not use a fireguard. It is vital to do so when a fire is lit in a room where there are children, or if you leave the fire unattended. Before leaving the house, be sure to put the fire out fully by pouring water over any embers that may still be burning.

LEFT
Behind a door wedged open with pebbles from Adour, a basket is filled with grape shoots and firewood that will be used to start fires.

RIGHT-HAND PAGE
It is not necessary to hide your reserve of winter logs. Crude wood gives a different aspect to this dignified room, evoking a Venetian palace.

Perfumes and scents

∾ *Our own scent is exclusive to us, just like our fingerprints: we may use the same perfume as the next person but our individual body chemistry modifies it, creating our own unique scent.*

It is the same with houses. You have only to open up a house that has been uninhabited for a long time, in the countryside, in town or by the seaside, to detect a scent that is its very own, which impregnates clothes, furniture and objects with such strength that the imprint sometimes takes years to fade.

Just as we arrange flowers around the house, we can fill it with different aromas to suit each room and each season. Use spice and wood scents in winter; fruit and flower fragrances for a bedroom; leaf, herb and citrus fruit perfumes in summer. ∾

Room fragrances

∾ If you like the smell of fruit in autumn, place a quince to ripen on a shelf or on top of a wardrobe. The room will be filled with an amber and fruity perfume.

∾ Room incense is easy to use; it quickly fills the room with the scent of your choice. To prevent it from exploding, never put the diffusing ring or the incense in direct contact with a hot bulb.

∾ Scented candles are also very pleasant. Do not place hot glass candle pots on a cold glass surface, as this may cause the glass to break. Cut the wick regularly as the candle melts and becomes smaller, and re-center it.

The scent of oranges and lemons

∾ In winter keep orange and lemon peel. If your cooker is equipped with electrical plates, place the peel on them on a very low heat. Their wondrous aroma will then pervade your kitchen.

ABOVE
A scented miscellany enclosed in an embroidered handkerchief may be used to perfume a drawer, or set on a bedside table.

Scents to keep pests away

Certain plants have been used for generations to keep away insects, especially mosquitoes.

∾ To keep mosquitoes away in Landes and Provence, they place potted basil or rose geranium on window sills.

∾ Our grandmothers used to coat window and mirror frames with onion juice to ensure that flies would not land on them.

∾ In Spain, during the summer, bowls with half-lemons studded with cloves are placed around food shops to keep flies at bay.

∾ The traditional remedy for deterring mosquitoes is to place a saucer filled with citronella oil in a room. Its pungent smell keeps them away. Be careful not to get it in direct contact with the skin, as it burns.

Pot-pourris

In England, the invention of endless varieties of pot-pourris has been elevated to a real art, with combinations of many different types of petals, leaves, bark, roots and fruit.

Green pot-pourri

ABOUT 50G (2OZ) EACH OF:

VERVAIN, LEMONGRASS, ROSEMARY,

MINT, LEMONBALM, SAGE,

PELARGONIUM, LIME AND LEMON PEEL

2 CINNAMON STICKS

1 VANILLA POD

3 DROPS LAVENDER OIL

3 DROPS OF SEVILLE ORANGE OR

NEROLI OIL

7.5ML (1½TSP) GRATED NUTMEG

7.5ML (1½TSP) WHOLE CLOVES

Mix all the ingredients in a bowl. To decorate, add flower petals of different colors.

ABOVE
An efficient wasp trap: simply pour sweet water into a glass globe. Inquisitive wasps will be imprisoned.

RIGHT-HAND PAGE
A pot-pourri of scented leaves and flower petals; the mixture can be altered as the seasons change.

Flowers and bouquets

Flowers are the most beautiful way to let nature enter your home bringing both color and scent. Gardeners know it is not a waste to cut a rose, dahlia or simple geranium flower for indoor display. Indeed, soon another flower, even sturdier than its predecessor, will grow where the cutting was taken from the garden...

Fresh flowers

Always add a drop of bleach to the vase water to keep the stems as fresh as possible. Change the water every day if you can.

To give more vigor to a bouquet that looks droopy, wrap it tightly in newspaper and place it in a bucket full of warm water for a few minutes. Then fill the bucket with very cold water and leave the bouquet for at least an hour.

Do not pick dahlias before they have blossomed, as they will struggle to do so once cut.

Poppies and cornflowers will keep longer if you burn the end of the stalk with the flame of a candle or a lighter.

Violets will wither less quickly if you dip the flowers in cool water. Spray them regularly with water as well.

To prevent lilies leaving stains of yellow powdery pollen on furniture or tablecloths, simply cut the stamens out with small scissors before arranging.

Tulips, narcissi and others

In order to extend the life of flowers such as narcissi and daffodils prick their stalks with a pin so they absorb water more easily and last longer.

LEFT-HAND PAGE
Once cut, violets do not absorb water through their stems, so spray them with water at least once a day to make them last longer. You can also put them in the fridge during the night.

ABOVE
Christmas roses, or hellebores, will last well in a vase, as long as the room is not too warm. Weather permitting, put them outside at night.

∾ Anemones, tulips, hyacinths, narcissi and hellebores do not like warm indoor environments. Unless frost has been forcast, you will help them to last longer by putting them outside at night.

Hard-stemmed flowers

∾ Hard-stemmed flowers such as roses, lilac, chrysanthemum, prunus and forsythia have to be treated so their stems can absorb water: in order to do this crush the end with a hammer, or split them into four with secateurs.

∾ To give your home the atmosphere of spring in winter, just cut a selection of cherry, prunus, forsythia or viburnum branches. Arranged together in a vase filled with water, they will produce light soft green leaves first, then their flowers will blossom in the warmth of the house.

BELOW
Picked in winter,
viburnum branches will
blossom in the house,
producing delicate
light green flowers.

RIGHT-HAND PAGE
Cultivated poppy stems should
be burned to stop the sap from
running and to prolong their
life. Wild poppies should be
treated in the same way.

Drying flowers and leaves

∾ The simplest and most effective way to create dried bouquets of flowers is to dry them away from sunlight and humidity.

∾ To speed the drying process you can use an oven on a very low setting. This works particularly well when drying roses.

∾ You can simply hang your flowers, tied in bouquets, on an old partitioning screen or a clothes horse. When hung in this fashion they become a decoration too, and look glorious in a living-room or a bedroom.

Digitalis infusion for bouquets

115G (4OZ) FRESHLY CUT
DIGITALIS LEAVES
1L (1¾PT) WATER

1. Heat the water and add in the leaves once it starts boiling. Then leave the mixture to infuse for a few minutes.

2. When the infusion is cold, bottle it and keep it in a cool place.

3. Mix this infusion with fresh vase water (⅔ water for ⅓ infusion) and your cut flowers will then keep for longer.

An old fashioned method for drying flowers is to lay some very fine sand, white and powdery like flour, at the bottom of a box sufficiently long and deep to contain the flowers and branches. Place your flowers on top and cover with a thick layer of sand. Close the box, store it away from the damp and wait about fifteen days. When the flowers are really dry, the petals will be "crunchy".

The stems of dried flowers are often fragile. You can replace them with florist's wire.

BELOW
The wooden frame of an old partitioning screen is turned into a practical and decorative support to dry bouquets during summer.

RIGHT-HAND PAGE
Silica gel from florists helps to dry all sorts of flowers while keeping their shape intact and their colors bright.

Drying leaves

2 PARTS WATER

1 PART GLYCERINE

(AVAILABLE FROM CHEMISTS)

1. Bring the water to a boil and pour in the glycerine. Leave to cool.
2. Dip the leaves in the glycerine solution.
3. Leave to dry but note that drying time varies. The leaves are ready when they look waxy. This method darkens the colour of plants. The most beautiful leaves to dry are those of oak or maple trees, which have luxurious golden or red tones. You can also dry beech, magnolia or boxtree branches by this method.

Furniture, wooden and parquet floors

∽ The smell of waxed wood and furniture symbolizes the order and perfection in houses like those we admire in paintings of Flemish masters. To give shine to furniture and wooden floors, nothing beats old-fashioned recipes based on honey-scented beeswax. But one can also appreciate the smooth and natural look of naked wood, simply washed, which through the months and years acquires a soft pale ash color, evoking images of boat decks cleaned every day with bucketfuls of water. ∽

Wooden furniture

∽ When a piece of furniture or a drawer does not close properly, the problem can be solved by rubbing the partitions with dry household soap.

∽ To stop water staining waxed wood, then rub it as soon as the water is spilt with cork, always in the direction of the grain.

∽ You can protect your furniture from insects and give it a lovely smell by smearing it regularly with lavender oil, a solution which acts as a powerful insecticide.

∽ Make a dust cloth by dipping a fine cotton cloth into a mixture of half water and half glycerine. This will attract dust and give shine to wood.

Natural flooring

An untreated, unwaxed, unvarnished wooden floor is a simple pleasure that everyone can enjoy. After many washes the wood becomes increasingly ash-colored and smooth when bleach is added to the soap used to clean it. The smell tends to linger in the house for an hour or two, but it is not necessary to use huge quantities of bleach.

Wood lovers may recommend that this treatment be used only on less valuable wooden floors made of pine or fir, and discourage its use on oak floors or other floors made of precious wood. But there is great outdoor nostalgia in the feel of wooden boards which look as if they have been exposed to the elements and washed repeatedly with gallons of water with a mop soaked thoroughly in a bucket. It is uplifting to walk barefoot on this clean-smelling wood.

Furniture wax

200G (7OZ) YELLOW WAX

200ML (7OZ) TURPENTINE OIL

50G (2OZ) WHITE SOAP

1. Coarsely grate the wax and soap.

2. Pour them into the turpentine and mix with a spatula.

3. When dissolved, pour the mixture into a glass jar clearly labelled.

For, strangely enough, the more that wood is washed, the more it becomes polished smooth and free of its splinters.

∾ If your wooden floor is waxed but you would prefer a "boat-deck" finish, strip or sand it down first before washing it daily, using bleach about twice a week.

Waxed wood

∾ Some people prefer the smell of waxed wood wafting through the house. You can create shiny floors reminiscent of those perfect examples in Flemish paintings by polishing them regularly. Those who do not have time to spare will simply use ready-made products to achieve this effect, but those who love tradition will go back to ancient recipes, based on beeswax with its incomparable smell.

∾ Avoid spray wax containing volatile silicones: they do no good to the wood, polishing it on the outside but drying it out inside.

Wooden floor wax

275G (10OZ) BEESWAX
275GML (10FL OZ) TURPENTINE

1. Coarsely grate the wax into a container that has a lid.
2. Dissolve the grated wax in the turpentine. This cold method takes longer but is less dangerous than using a bain-marie to heat the turpentine.
3. Stir the mixture frequently. If the result is not smooth enough, secure the lid on the container and dip in a large bowl of very hot water.

Paste for gold frames

To clean gold frames that do not have much value, use this old recipe.

1 EGG WHITE, WHISKED UNTIL STIFF
15ML (1TBSP) BLEACH

1. Mix the egg white and bleach together then gently brush onto the frame.
2. Leave for a few seconds.
3. Rinse with a damp sponge then polish with a fine cloth.

Soap wax

In the olden days, housewives also used polish made of soapy water and wax, which did not clog up the wood.

1L (1¾PT) HOT WATER
150G (5OZ) BEESWAX
15G (1TBSP) BLACK SOAP OR
HOUSEHOLD SOAP
45G (3TBSP) SODA CRYSTALS

1. Coarsely grate the wax and the soap.
2. Add them with the soda crystals to the hot water and then mix thoroughly.
3. Pour the mixture into an airtight container and label carefully.
This polish is brushed on still warm or slightly warmed up. Leave the wood to dry a few hours then rub with a cloth to make it shiny.

Sparkling tableware

In the past, housewives took great pride in their crockery and china cupboards, where dishes, soup tureens, plates, soup bowls and spotless, shiny glasses were stacked and stored in impeccable order.

At the turn of the twentieth century, the Countess of Gence, in her Encyclopaedia of Practical Life, *specified what a full and practical set of tableware should comprise of, for the benefit of young brides. According to her, it required at the very least "a dozen soup bowls, two dozen dinner plates, a dozen dessert plates, a soup tureen, a salad dish, two round shallow dishes, a round deep dish, an oval dish, a gravy boat with platter, two hors-d'oeuvre dishes, a vegetable dish, a fruit bowl, two cake stands." This abundance is explained by the strict rules that regulated tableware.*

And this is without mentioning the crystal ware, which included no fewer than one hundred glasses of different sizes and uses to serve water, Burgundy, Bordeaux, Madeira or Rhine wine, champagne or orangeade…Tumblers were reserved for lemonade or beer, small glasses for liqueurs, and six to eight pitchers were required.

Cutlery was less prodigious, but often included more than sixty silver or silver-plated (less expensive) items.

Knives

Before the advent of stainless steel, knife blades rusted easily, especially when they came in regular contact with acidic elements such as vinegar or lemon. This is why knives were never used to eat salad. This custom is still retained in some circles and is regarded as good manners.

To polish blades, it was usual to rub them with a cork dipped in polishing cream. To get rid of rust, they were simply planted in the ground!

Rub knife blades with the cut side of a potato dipped in Tripoli powder (polishing powder) mixed with bicarbonate of soda. Leave the knives to dry and then rub with a fine cloth.

If you use a knife to cut fish, garlic or onion, dip the blade in hot ashes to remove the smell.

Tableware

When cutlery was monogrammed in France, the owner's initials were on the reverse side. In England, the opposite applied. This explains why the French always lay their forks with the prongs on the table-cloth, whereas the English do the opposite.

In general old, horn-rimmed cutlery must not be washed in a dishwasher. Instead clean it in warm water, as the horn splits when placed in hot water. From time to time, rub it with a cloth imbued with olive oil to impart shine. This advice also applies to knives with mother-of-pearl or ebony handles.

Washing valuable glassware

It is best to wash old crystal glasses by hand, as the dishwasher may dull them irreparably.

~ To avoid cracking or chipping a glass, our forebears used to put a cloth or dish towel at the bottom of their washing-up basin. This method also applies to china and faïence ware.

~ Use newspaper sheets cut into small pieces to clean glass. The oil used to make printing ink gives newspaper its cleaning properties. Put some pieces in the item to be cleaned then fill up with water. Shake thoroughly then rinse under very hot water.

~ If the glass is filthy, add a little fine sand to the water and shake vigorously to get rid of all the dirt.

~ If a bottle is used to store oil or any other greasy liquid, fill it up with warm coffee grounds diluted in water. This cleans and deodorizes at the same time. This method is also ideal for cleaning a scent bottle.

Sticking labels
on glass the easy way

~ If you want to stick a label on a bottle, jar, pot or flask without using glue, there is a simple method you can follow: dip the label in a saucer filled with milk then stick it immediately on to the glass. Smooth with a damp sponge or fine cloth to get rid of air bubbles, and wash off any traces of milk. Then simply write on the required information

Returning the shine to glasses, bottles and pitchers

6 EGG SHELLS

JUICE OF 2 LEMONS

OR ½ GLASS OF VINEGAR

1. Break the egg shells into tiny pieces and put them in the glass items that require cleaning.
2. Pour in the lemon juice or vinegar and shake.
3. Leave overnight, so the shells dissolve. If necessary, use a bottle brush to clean the dirtiest areas. Empty out the solution.
4. Rinse in very hot water.

RIGHT
To stick a label on a bottle, there is no need for glue. Simply smear the paper with milk and affix it immediately with a damp cloth or sponge.

RIGHT-HAND PAGE
With a dish towel at the bottom of a basin. It is safe to wash even the daintiest and most fragile glasses as you will not stretch or chip them.

Kitchen utensils

In Provence, where cooking was done with earthenware dishes and utensils, housewives used to rub a garlic clove dipped in olive oil on the outside base of frying-pans, pots, fondue pots and heatproof or ovenproof dishes. After this treatment, the earthenware resisted heat perfectly.

An old Alsace trick to make earthenware pots hold liquid without leaking was to fill the receptacle with boiling milk and leave it overnight. The following day, all they had to do was rinse it and the pot would be totally leak-proof.

Horsetail (*Equisetum arvense*) is a plant native to the Mediterranean that loves damp places. Its slightly knotty main stem bears thin and spindly stalks. Its distinctive feature is that it contains silica, like sand, which is why in rural areas it was used in the past to scrub metal and pans.

∾ To make a traditional vegetable pad, take a handful of marsh horsetail. Make a braid with the stalks to obtain a pad, which you can then use to scrub metal pans and utensils.

∾ If you cannot find a source of horsetail, order "mock bamboo" from your florist. It is a Japanese horsetail that works just as well.

∾ However, it is best to use true marsh horsetail to polish metal, whereas the thicker florist's horsetail is better for scrubbing metals stained by flames or fat.

Putting away your tableware

∾ Use silk paper to protect old tableware (plates, cups, china or enamelled dishes) which are especially dear to you. A single sheet of silk paper between each item will stop them from damaging each other through close contact.

∾ If you break one or more plates, do not worry about having tableware that does not match. Instead have fun finding plates of similar colours or shapes, or go for opposite or different shades, alternating the plates on your table.

LEFT-HAND PAGE
Stems of florist's horsetail (mock bamboo) can be broken into small pieces and used as a pad to scrub the base of even the dirtiest of pans.

RIGHT
The Provençal way to "harden" the bottom of earthenware dishes, to be used on the cooker or in the oven, is to rub them with raw garlic and then olive oil.

Clean and beautiful

∾ *The objects that surround us in our homes deserve our regular attention. From the humblest to the most precious object, they can become colorful and shiny in our hands, thanks to those recipes that are often passed on from mother to daughter. In this way, we learn to value the traditional properties of Spanish or Meudon white, whose origins remain a mystery. Why was this product, used in the past for the daily care of metal and glass, given this double attribution? It still remains a mystery at the start of the new millennium...*∾

Sparkling metal

∾ In winter, when you are using open fires to warm your home, keep the ash from the fire and mix it to a paste with a little oil. This combination is excellent for gently cleaning aluminium or stainless-steel pans, as well as pewter and iron items.

Bronze

∾ Bronze can simply be cleaned with soapy water. If the piece is outside, such as a letterbox or door stop, you can protect it with a layer of wax, which will also give it a nice shine.

∾ Golden bronze can be cleaned with the same product that is suitable for silver: Spanish white diluted in methylated spirits and water.

Silver

∾ Dull-looking silver will regain its shine if you put it in a pan of water in which you have already heated a piece of aluminium foil.

∾ The cooking water of peeled potatoes is excellent for giving silver back its shine. You can also rub the object with the pulp of a boiled potato.

LEFT-HAND PAGE
Salt, flour and lemon juice (or white vinegar) are all you need to clean the dirtiest of copper objects.

ABOVE
A copper door knocker will keep its shine and sheen with a thin layer of wax and regular polishing with a soft cloth.

Silverware paste

This traditional recipe was used in the past to clean silver or silver-plated objects.

30ML (2TBSP) METHYLATED SPIRITS
15ML (1TBSP) SPANISH (MEUDON) WHITE

1. Soak a fine cloth, with a soft texture that will not scratch metal, in the mixture of Spanish white and methylated spirits. For chiselled objects, use a small soft flexible brush in order to clean hidden crevices.
2. Leave the mixture to dry, then rub with a clean cloth or chamois cloth to give a beautiful shine.
If the mixture is left in the chiselling, clean it off by rubbing with pure alcohol or lemon juice.

ABOVE
Our ancestors discovered that sorrel leaves are nature's excellent cleaning agents for pewter.

RIGHT-HAND PAGE
Knife blades and silverware regain their shine when cleaned with a traditional paste made with Spanish (Meudon) white.

Copper

෴ Lemon juice brushed on copper is often enough to clean it, however dirty, and give it lustre.
෴ Fresh sorrel leaves, and the green leaves of leeks, make copper and pewter gleam.
෴ To give extra shine to cleaned copper, expose it to sunlight for a few hours.
෴ Copper will keep its shine for longer if you finish polishing with a ball of newspaper sheets.

Mirrors and windows

෴ Wet newspaper rolled into a ball will clean windows superlatively.

Copper paste

JUICE OF 1 LEMON
30G (3TBSP) PLAIN FLOUR
25G (1TBSP) FINE SALT

1. Prepare a paste with all the ingredients.
2. Apply it to the copper with a soft flexible brush or a soft cloth.
3. Leave to take effect for a few minutes.
4. Rinse with clean water then buff to a shine using your usual copper-polishing product.

Baskets and straw or wicker objects

∾ To dust and clean basketware, do not hesitate to use a hose pipe (in the bath or in the garden) once or twice a year, then leave the baskets to dry outside.

∾ A straw mat will last longer if you wash it in hot salted water. To protect it from dust afterwards, smear it with a thin layer of wax and rub it with a soft cloth to give it shine.

∾ Cane chairs often go out of shape. To restore their shape, wet the back of the cane thoroughly with boiling water, then leave it to dry as quickly as possible in the sun or near a source of heat.

Rugs

Methods used in the past to freshen up rugs sometimes seemed eccentric. After dusting the rug, some people sprinkled it with tea leaves or damp coffee grounds to revive the colors. A cabbage cut in half was slid across the whole surface of the rug, and cut again as its leaves absorbed the dirt.

∾ To revive the colors of your rugs, add 10ml (2tsp) ammoniac to 1l (1¾pt) of water and scrub the whole of the rug surface gently with a sponge soaked in this liquid. Then dry the rug with a dry cloth.

∾ In winter, if it is snowing, you can cover the rug with a fine layer of snow and brush it straight away, or scrub it directly with a compact snowball.

∾ Add a teaspoon of ammoniac to 1l (1¾pt) of water and wet a fine cloth in this mixture. Apply it briefly to windows and mirrors, which will ensure that they regain their brilliant shine.

∾ Never wash windows when the sun is shining: the cleaning agent will leave white marks as it dries.

∾ Methylated spirits can economically replace any shop products.

∾ To give a perfect shine to their windows and mirrors, professional window cleaners would use a mixture of water, Spanish white and methylated spirits in equal quantities.

∾ To stop steam from collecting on a kitchen or bathroom mirror, a simple technique is to rub the glass with a fine cloth imbued with glycerine. Then give it a shine with a clean cloth.

∾ You can get the same result by using dry household soap instead of glycerine.

ABOVE
Choose a fine sunny day to
wash and dry wicker
and straw objects in the
open air.

RIGHT-HAND PAGE
This large mirror sparkled
again after having been
smeared with a paste made of
Spanish (Meudon) white.

THE LINEN
cupboard

*N*obody has ever conjured up the closed universe of a wardrobe and the place it occupies in a house better than Henri Bergson, in his *La Poétique de L'Espace* (*Poetry of Space*). The philosopher quotes the words of Milosz who said that: "the wardrobe is full of the silent tumult of our memories."

"Is there anyone sensitive to the poetic quality of words who will not react to the word 'wardrobe'..? Anyone who is sensitive to antique furniture...knows instinctively that the inside space of an old wardrobe is deep. It is an intimate space, one that does not open up to just anybody...Only a fool would put any old thing in a wardrobe...In the wardrobe, lives are ordered to protect the house against total chaos. There, order is king, or rather order is a kingdom. Order pays hommage to the wardrobe's family history."

Do we still have time today to spend hours washing, ironing, folding and putting away the linen of which our ancestors were so proud? The interior of a wardrobe, fragrant with wax, was protected from dust with sheets of paper, and piles of linen were tied with ribbons. As soon as you opened the doors you could smell lavender, picked in summer and enclosed in small sachets wedged between piles of linen.

Washing, drying and ironing

An essential activity in daily life, laundering used to be surrounded by beliefs and superstitions. Often it was thought that you could not do the laundry inside a house where a sick person or a pregnant lady lived as this could bring bad luck to the household. On certain days and during some periods of the year laundry was forbidden: the Advent period, the days between Christmas and New Year, Holy Week, the month of the dead (November), the Assumption or the Day of Purification of the Virgin Mary, not forgetting Good Friday, or during a woman's menstruation when she is considered traditionally impure... Transgressing these taboos would bring ill fortune.

Keeping clothes white

Add lemon peel secured in a cloth bag to the washing for whiter underwear.

Add a glass of water with 30 per cent hydrogen peroxide to rinsing water for whiter than white clothes.

Vinegar can be used to neutralize washing powder that foams too much: just add a few spoonfuls or a small glassful, according to the quantity of water used to stop uncontrollable overflowing and let the powder's cleaning powers take effect.

Delicates

To wash silk, wool and dark delicate textiles, use ivy, Panama wood or beer leaves.

Our grandmothers sometimes used the cooking water of dried haricot beans to wash light cotton fabrics and silk or cotton muslin.

In the past, stout beer was used to clean black lace, such as Chantilly.

You can also prepare a mixture of soapwort root, a small wildflower that grows on slopes and in fields.

Washing powder for very dirty clothes

When clothes were extremely soiled, then they would be soaked in a soda-crystal-based solution. This was reserved for strong textiles that did not run.

1 GLASS OF HOUSEHOLD SOAP FLAKES

1 GLASS OF SODA CRYSTALS

10ML (2TSP) LAVENDER OR ROSEMARY
ESSENTIAL OIL

1. Add all the ingredients to very hot water and mix until dissolved.
2. Soak the clothes overnight.
3. Rinse thoroughly with clean water.

Its five-petalled flowers are light pink. Washerwomen and drapers used it often, as its leaves and even more its roots, rich in saponin, make the water foam and render it an ideal detergent for delicate textiles; it is in fact still used today by specialists to clean old fabrics at the Victoria & Albert Museum, in London. If you cannot find any soapwort near you, buy crushed roots from a herbalist.

~ Another product that we no longer use to clean fabric is bran. Add a fistful to 1l (1¾pt) water. Bran water was used to wash colored and delicate fabrics.

ABOVE
A black linen shirt washed in a traditional infusion of ivy leaves is dried in the shade, out of direct sunlight.

RIGHT-HAND PAGE
Our grandmothers used the rhizomes of the iris to give washed clothes a light violet scent.

Ivy water

Ivy water was used to clean delicates such as silk, wool and black or dark linen.

115G (4OZ) IVY LEAVES
1L (1¾PT) WATER

1. Prepare the concoction by boiling the ivy leaves in the water for a few minutes.
2. Wet the clothes before putting them in the ivy and water preparation.
3. Leave to cool then scrub gently before rinsing in clean water.

Old-fashioned soapwort water

115G (4OZ) SOAPWORT ROOT,
IN CHUNKS
1.5L (2½PT) WATER

1. Start by soaking the soapwort in the water overnight.
2. The following day, boil the water gently for 15 minutes. Then drain the mixture, reserving the water.
3. Pour 500ml (16fl oz) of water on the fresh cooked soapwort and then boil again for another 5 minutes.
4. Filter, then mix the two liquids. Simply stir the water to make it foam. You can replace the soapwort with the same amount of Panama wood cut into small chunks.

Tough stains

～ Scrub the stain with slightly damp household soap. Leave to take effect overnight then wash as usual.

～ In the past, to get rid of an ink or fruit stain on white fabric, sorrel salt or oxalic acid was used. This aggressive treatment must be carried out with care, because if the agent stays in contact with the fabric for too long, it can make a hole: wet the stained area, then sprinkle it lightly with salt or acid and let it take effect for a few seconds. Rinse thoroughly.

～ Rust or blood stains disappear or fade if you wet them thoroughly with the juice of rhubarb stems or sorrel leaves (just blend them). Then wash as usual.

～ You can also get rid of a blood stain by wetting it with 10 per cent hydrogen peroxide or pure lemon juice. Then wash as usual.

～ When old linen has reddish-brown stains or marks, soak it in raw fresh milk (our grandmothers used whey or what they called "pestle" milk), and expose it to sunlight before washing as usual.

～ If red wine is spilled on a tablecloth, sprinkle it immediately with fine salt. Even if most of it is absorbed, this is still not enough to make the stain vanish. Try to dampen it with white wine, white alcohol (vodka or eau-de-vie) or simply with methylated spirits. Wash straight away.

Dry cleaning with flour

～ To clean delicate and light-colored fabrics that you do not want to wash in water, especially woollens, you can use plain flour or cornflour. Place the clothing in a basin, cover it with flour and rub gently so that the flour penetrates well. Leave overnight, then brush and beat the clothing with a fine bamboo cane or a rug beater.

Scented clothes

～ If you need to boil soiled white fabrics, add Florence iris rhizomes to the water to give them a marvellous yet subtle violet scent. You can obtain these rare rhizomes from certain herbalists.

～ You can replace perfumed softeners, which are often too harsh, with the same measure of spirit vinegar. To give your clothes a delightful fragrance, add a few drops of your favourite essential oil such as lavender, vervain or rosemary to the vinegar. You can also add some essential oil to the iron water (one drop is ample). Or try adding a teaspoon of rose water, orange flower water, or lavender, sage or basil water.

Drying clothes

In the countryside clothes used to be dried flat on the grass and bleached in the meadow for three days. The combined action of sun, moon and morning dew was thought to give clothes an incomparable whiteness. Moreover, it has now been proven that the sun has beneficial disinfecting properties.

LEFT-HAND PAGE
The juice extracted from rhubarb (or sorrel) stems contains a substance that can get rid of rust or blood stains on fabrics.

In Holland, for want of sun, indigo or pastel blue was used very early on to give clothes a much sought-after sky-blue tone. This habit spread throughout Europe: not so long ago, a "blue bag" was still one of the essential accessories of a good housewife. The small cloth bag was pressed by hand in a basin of water. When the water was the desired tone, clean clothes were soaked in it, then squeezed and left to dry.

In any very cold winter weather, to prevent any clothes drying outside from becoming stiff, add a fistful of coarse salt to the last rinsing water.

Always turn colored clothes inside out before drying them outside otherwise, the color will fade in the sun. Delicate colors must be left to dry in the shade.

Rubbing terry towels gently between your hands will restore their softness, lost during washing.

Ironing

To dampen clothes before ironing, spray water on them then roll them up into balls so that the moisture spreads throughout the fabric.

If the iron sole is dirty, rub it with half a lemon sprinkled with fine salt.

So the iron glides more easily, heat it slightly and smear candlewax on the sole. Wipe with a clean cloth.

To iron embroidered fabric or clothes without the embroidered patterns being imprinted, simply place a towel under the embroidery.

You will achieve an impeccable crease in your trousers by slipping a piece of craft paper inside the fabric. Another old trick is to rub the inside of the fabric with a piece of dry soap before pressing.

If an old fabric has lost its lustre, spray it with vinegared water and iron with a damp cloth that has also been dampened with vinegared water.

If you leave a hot iron too long on the same spot and it leaves a mark on the fabric, try to get it off immediately using the following mixture: an equal quantity of spirit vinegar, fine salt and soap flakes. Mix these ingredients and apply the paste to the fabric. Leave to take effect for a few minutes and rinse in warm water.

Old-fashioned starch

Rice water was a natural starch commonly used by our grandmothers, to starch delicate fabrics or shirt collars. Here is a simple recipe for a laundry dressing.

115G (4OZ) STARCH

1L (1¾PT) HOT WATER

40G (1½OZ) GUM ARABIC

1. Dissolve the starch in the hot water.

2. Add the gum arabic and stir thoroughly.

3. Soak the fabric or clothes that require starching in this mixture.

In the past, so that starched clothes would not stick to the iron, laundrywomen would add a pinch of salt to the starch.

RIGHT-HAND PAGE
Clothes will smell wonderful if you replace the distilled water used in a steam iron with lavender, orange flower or rose water.

Traditional dyes

∾ If you love experimenting with colors, you will enjoy using plants that have been known for centuries for their dyeing properties: the red fleshy root of the madder gives all manner of red tones; the tropical plant indigo and the woad plant yield blue tones; gall nuts dye black; weld obtained from the plant dyer's rocket, curcumin or saffron give yellow dyes (saffron was still commonly used in the Pithiviers region, near Paris, up to the beginning of the twentieth century). Many plants traditionally used for making dyes are being cultivated again and some herbalists and specialist shops stock them. ∾

Reviving tired colors

∾ To revive white linen that has become slightly yellowed, just dye it with natural colorings such as tea, lime-blossom infusion or even chicory, made into a concoction. This will enhance it with a more or less strong highlights.

∾ It is not widely known that henna or onion peel, used in large quantities (at least 115g (4oz) per 1l (1¾pt) water), give lovely reddish-brown colors. Alternatively, use beetroot or blueberry juice, which give subtle rose or purple-blue shades.

∾ The fabrics you intend to dye must first be washed thoroughly and then put wet into the dye water.

∾ Lemon juice brightens up red colors (use one glass of lemon juice per basin of water).

∾ Ammoniac brightens up dyes containing blues. Use 45ml (3tbsp) per 1l (1¾pt) of water.

LEFT-HAND PAGE
Blue bags with indigo powder, which our grandmothers used for bleaching and also to add sky-blue colour to fabrics.

Home-made dye

115G (4 OZ) PLANTS OR ROOTS FOR
1L (1¾PT) WATER
15-30ML (1-2TBSP) VINEGAR
OR LEMON JUICE

1. Enclose the plant matter in a muslin or canvas sachet. Put it, with the fabric to be dyed, in a pan filled with the water, and heat gently.

2. Stir the cloth in the liquid continuously during the dyeing time, to ensure it is well impregnated with the dye colors.

3. For a darker color, leave the fabric to soak overnight before rinsing.

4. Add 1 to 2 spoonfuls of vinegar or lemon juice to the last rinsing water to fix the dye.

Avoid using aluminium or copper pans, as these will alter the dye. Instead use enamelled metal or stainless-steel containers. You could also use an old clothes boiler if you need to heat large quantities of water.

Clothes and accessories

⟡ The fabrics and clothes that our grandmothers wore have such magical appeal. We have fond memories of curling up in a zenana dressing-gown (a thin rippled fabric used for making light clothes), or making a shirt out of silky nansouk or cotton batiste, or lounging in a matinée top (an unfitted, half-length blouse), with a dimity skirt (white cotton fabric) while sewing corozo buttons (made of a substance extracted from palm seeds) on a drill jacket. In the evening, a gauzy floss silk scarf would keep the neck warm... ⟡

Storing delicate clothes

⟡ Fold delicate clothes carefully between sheets of white silk paper and lay them in boxes, to prevent them from creasing and to keep out the dirt.

⟡ Silk or cashmere scarves, whose threads are very delicate, should be stored in a flat box or a large pretty envelope reserved specifically for them.

⟡ To prevent skirts and trousers from creasing when hung up in the wardrobe, cover hangers with padded cotton or with a cardboard cylinder cut to size.

Protection from insects

Before the advent of mothballs, our grandmothers used their own recipes to keep moths away. While lavender was the favorite, they also used a mixture of pyrethrum (a type of small wild chrysanthemum, which is still used today for its insecticidal properties), white pepper, patchouli roots (for the scent) and tobacco, with which they generously sprinkled their clothes before putting them away in their drawers and wardrobes.

LEFT-HAND PAGE
Silk or light woollen scarves are lovingly packed in boxes. With lids secured they are protected from dust.

ABOVE
Pepper corns placed in pockets and in the inner lining of clothes put away for summer will keep the moths away.

111

Our grandmothers used to hang sachets filled with camphor in the sleeves of clothes. They also made tinctures using rosemary and wild thyme, which they spread in cupboards and wardrobes; and sometimes they imitated the Russians, who used tincture of colocynth (the bark of these small gourd-like plants was cut into chunks and left to marinate in alcohol for several days). They often sprinkled the inner lining of their clothes with pepper before they put them away.

ᔫ Always wash woollen sweaters before putting them away in the wardrobe. Unlaundered woollen items attract moths, which love the human smell!

ᔫ When wool pills into balls, it is easy to get rid of these tiny balls by sliding a razor across the damaged surface. Do this with great care, so you do not cut the thread of the fabric.

Anti-moth sachets

25G (1OZ) GROUND PYRETHRUM

25G (1OZ) CRUSHED WHITE PEPPER

25G (1OZ) CRUSHED SANDALWOOD OR

PATCHOULI ROOT

25G (1OZ) GROUND CAMPHOR OR

TOBACCO

Mix all the ingredients together then put the powder in small sachets to go in drawers and wardrobes. You can also sprinkle the mixture directly on to clothes before putting them away for the winter or summer. If you cannot obtain sandalwood or patchouli root from a herbalist, use a few drops of their essential oils instead.

ᔫ You can also brush woollen clothes with a nail brush. However, the more you wash wool, the less it pills so it should be a short-term problem.

ᔫ If you pile shirts and blouses on a shelf, remember to place them head to tail so they do not fall over.

ᔫ A scented soap placed in a clothes cupboard will release a gentle fragrance.

Identifying fabrics

ᔫ Take a few threads from the hem of the garment and burn them slowly so that you can identify the fabric. If they are synthetic, they burn very quickly and seem to melt. Cotton threads burn quickly and without smell.

Hats

ᔫ A straw hat that has lost its shape will regain its original shape if it is wetted and then placed on a wooden ball or on your head to dry.

ᔫ A velvet hat that has been damaged by the rain will look smooth and glossy again if you expose it to the hot steam of a kettle for a few minutes. Then give shine to the velvet by brushing it with a soft brush in the direction of the pile.

Shoes

It is men, curiously enough, who seem to take the best care of their shoes. Having chosen them with great care, some spend hours maintaining them, ensuring that their shoes age beautifully.

ᔫ A lovely shine is obtained by spreading a "scumble," rather than a thick layer of polish, on the leather. It is best to use a synthetic sponge reserved for this purpose. Wet it in hot water (which is better than spitting on the shoe). Soak it with shoe polish and cover the shoe with a very thin layer of polish. Leave to dry and then shine with a soft cloth.

Wet shoes should be stuffed with newspaper and left to dry away from any source of heat; otherwise, the leather will harden and it could crack when the shoes are worn again.

Taking care of patent leather

45ML (3TBSP) CRÈME FRÂICHE

10ML (2TSP) FLAX OIL

1. Mix the crème frâiche and oil together and then spread a thin layer on the patent leather.
2. Leave to dry, then rub gently with a fine wool cloth to make the leather shine.

Cleaning straw hats

15–20G (⅔–¾OZ) OXALIC ACID

1 GLASS OF WATER OR JUICE OF 1 LEMON

1. Mix the acid with the water or lemon juice. Scrub the straw with a soft brush dipped in the mixture.
2. Leave to take effect for a few minutes, then rinse with clean water.
3. Leave to dry in the open air.
For cleaning white straw, use neat lemon juice and then expose the hat to sunlight.

You can make shoes shine even more by rubbing the cut side of a lemon all over the shoe before the final polishing stage.

There is nothing to equal a traditional, quality polish. Even if silicone shoe polishes can make leather shine in record time, it is best not to use them too often, as the leather will eventually become dry and crack. If the polish starts to dry up, just warm it up in a bain-marie or dilute it with some lemon juice, vinegar or turpentine.

Patent-leather shoes can be kept in good condition by cleaning them with a fine cloth soaked in milk, crème fraîche or petroleum jelly.

To give the velvety appearance back to suede-look leather, simply rub it gently with a light-colored scouring pad (ordinary green pads could leave smears, especially on light leather). You can also use very fine-grade sandpaper.

ABOVE
To give your shoes an incomparable shine, rub them with the cut side of a lemon then polish with a cloth.

RIGHT-HAND PAGE
An old armchair, rejuvenated with a coat of paint, provides a picturesque setting for some splendid straw hats.

To make leather soles water resistant, coat them regularly with hot flax oil, using a brush.

Flax oil brushed over the sole will also stop shoes from squeaking.

Shoes left in a damp place can become stained with mould, but this is easily removed with a cloth dampened with turpentine.

Gloves

In the past, going out without gloves or a hat was unheard of. Made of leather or glazed leather (cotton gloves were kept for summer), they were looked after with great care.

Leather gloves were simply rubbed with breadcrumbs. These can be replaced today by a special rubber used for nubuck leather. Glazed leather gloves were gently rubbed with a flannel pad soaked with benzine.

Washable gloves can be cleaned in soapy water to which a few drops of glycerine have been added to soften the leather. Put on the gloves and scrub them gently. Rinse them in warm water.

Keep delicate gloves in a special box, between sheets of silk paper. If you wish, put scented plants such as sprigs of rosemary, or perfumed talcum powder at the bottom of the box.

Cuddly toys

Soft toys must not be put in a washing machine, unless they are labelled washable. However, they often need a good clean, especially when continuously cuddled and dragged around by a child.

Rejuvenate them by putting them in a polythene bag half filled with cornflour or talcum powder. Close the bag and shake thoroughly. Then simply brush them to get rid of the powder.

Cleaning with talcum powder is also good for fur accessories, such as a neck wrap, boa, pill-box hat or bonnet. Always brush with a slightly hard brush. If the fur is light-colored and stained, dilute a small spoonful of talcum powder or flour in two spoonfuls of mineral oil and use this paste to cover the stained area. Leave it to dry and then brush it gently off.

LEFT-HAND PAGE
Scented peel, bark, flowers or leaves impart their beautiful aroma to a pair of cherished leather gloves.

OPPOSITE
No need to subject teddy to a bath: a small amount of talcum powder, a good brushing and the dirt will disappear.

BEAUTY
and well-being

*A*t a time when perfumeries and drug stores offer the most elaborate and sophisticated products, natural recipes nevertheless have an important role to play. The science and technology used to make essential oils, creams, balms or other remedies relies more and more often on traditions borrowed from ancient civilizations. Equipped with the secrets that our ancestors passed down from one generation to another, cosmetologists today draw on the properties of plants or simple components such as milk, oil or honey.

Health through plants

~ *The secrets of promoting beauty and health through the use of plants have been known since ancient times. Herbal remedies and beauty creams were extensively used in all civilizations, including those of India, China, Greece and Rome. In Ancient Egypt "ladies of high society used sweet almond oil, honey or cinnamon-based ointments," and ordinary ladies used simple mint or thyme-scented oils" (Thomas de Quincey,* La Toilette de la Dame Hébraïque, *(The Toilet of the Hebrew Lady) Editions du Promeneur, 1992).*

Lavender, thyme, rosemary, sage, garlic, rose and lilies have been grown in gardens since the beginning of time, for both their aesthetic appeal and the well-being they dispense. ~

Thyme against the common cold

~ When you are coming down with a cold, ward it off by sipping a thyme infusion every hour, sweetened with clear honey and with a slice of lemon and two cloves added.

~ Place a few drops of thyme essential oil on your handkerchief and on your pillow; this will aid your breathing at night.

Lily oil

This oil will clean your face and heal small burns.

110G (4OZ) FRESHLY PICKED MADONNA
LILY PETALS,
120ML (4FL OZ) SWEET ALMOND OIL

1. Leave the petals to marinate in the oil for about 15 days.
2. Filter, bottle and label clearly.

Lily for the skin

Lilies were grown in cloisters during the Middle Ages, not only because they symbolized the purity of the Virgin Mary but also because they were mentioned among the plants of the "*Capitularis de Villis,*" a definitive directory of all the plants that were good for curing mild daily aches and pains, and which the Emperor Charlemagne recommended should be grown in the gardens of his empire.

~ Lilies are friends of the skin, which they help to heal. Use their petals or bulbs boiled in milk. Once puréed, these will help to relieve skin problems such as dermatitis or other minor irritations.

Mint for dogs

One mint in particular, *Mentha Pulegia,* owes its name to the fact that since ancient times it has been thought to keep fleas away (in Latin *pulegia* means "flea").

~ In the olden days, farmers never forgot to mix a few sprigs of mint into mattress linings, and always put a thick layer of it in dogs' kennels, which were often riddled with fleas.

St John's Wort oil

115G (4OZ) FRESHLY PICKED ST JOHN'S
WORT FLOWERS
120ML (4FL OZ) OLIVE OIL

1. Put the flowers and the oil in a closed container and leave to marinate for at least 15 days, preferably in the sun.
2. Filter, bottle and label the preparation, which will now have an amazing dark red color.

Sage to counter perspiration

∾ Pick sage leaves and let them dry. Grind them, then mix them into medicated talcum powder to use under the armpits and on your feet.

∾ You can also use this powder inside your shoes (especially sneakers) as a deodorant.

∾ Alternatively, simply put a bouquet of sage leaves in your shoes.

Properties of St John's Wort

In the countryside, in the olden days, St John's Wort oil was a favorite, being one of the simplest and most used family remedies.

An astonishing purple color, it is used to massage aches and pains away and especially to promote the healing process of the skin after a minor burn or injury. It was also used in the Middle Ages to ward off evil spirits...

We know now that St John's Wort has invaluable anti-inflammatory, healing and antiseptic properties.

Lemon for the throat

Lemon is traditionally used to soothe sore throats, as it is rich in vitamin C and fights off infections.

∾ It is best to use hot or warm lemon juice and to strengthen its soothing action by sweetening it with clear honey.

Remedies for insect bites and stings

∾ If you have been stung by a bee in the countryside, choose four different herbs and rub them firmly on the bite. Plantain, recognizable by its large oval and ribbed leaves and its small puff-like green flowers at the end of a long stem, is one of the most soothing herbs.

∾ Vinegar, and lemon, onion or leek juice also soothe insect bites and stings.

Refined toiletries

❧ Just as much as fine clothes and jewellery, perfumes and other cosmetics have always featured large among the plays of seduction...

In his small book devoted to La Toilette de la Dame Hébraïque (The Toilet of the Hebrew Lady), *published by Editions du Promeneur in 1992, the English writer Thomas de Quincey describes an accessory that was worn as a necklace by the aristocratic ladies of Ancient Palestine. It was a "small finely crafted box, made of silver or gold, or sometimes a dazzling white onyx phial, filled with the rarest perfumes and fragrant spices of the Orient", including musk, myrrh, rose oil and rose water. Worn continuously, this object perfumed both the skin and clothes. ❧*

Tailor-made soap

❧ If you have sensitive skin, buy a hypo-allergenic soap-free bar, as soap can irritate some skins. It is available in most drug stores.

❧ Do not throw away your soap leftovers: grate them and use the flakes to make a new soap that you can perfume and color (using food colorings that will not cause allergies) according to your taste.

Old-fashioned soap

115G (4OZ) GOOD QUALITY SOAP

7.5ML (1½TSP) ALMOND OIL

2.5ML (½TSP) BERGAMOT OIL

(OR LEMON, NEROLI, MANDARIN OR ANY

OTHER FRUIT OF THE SAME FAMILY)

45ML (3TBSP) ORANGE FLOWER WATER OR

DISTILLED WATER

1. Grate the soap into flakes and put in a food processor.

2. Add the almond and bergamot oil, or other oil of your choice. Then pour in the orange flower water or distilled water and transfer the mixture to a pan.

3. Heat gently until the soap has completely melted. If you wish to color your soap, add some food coloring to the pan.

4. Pour the hot liquid into previously oiled moulds, and leave in a cool place until the soap has hardened. Alternatively, wait until the soap mixture thickens and then shape it by hand into small balls for guest soap or larger ones for bath soap.

Add honey, oats or bran 115g (4oz) for 115g (4oz) of soap, to this basic recipe if you wish.

Facial care

∽ Egg yolk applied to the face cleans thoroughly and leaves the skin smooth and silky.

∽ If your skin is greasy, you can use honey (clear or set) as a cleanser. Smear your face with honey and massage gently with your fingertips. Then rinse with pure water or flower water (rose, orange flower, witch hazel or any other).

∽ You can also mix honey with rose water in equal quantities. This mixture will give you a lotion with a lovely perfume that is ideal for skins that tend to be greasy or combination.

∽ Half a pot of yogurt beaten with one or two drops of sweet almond oil or any other sweet oil (jojoba, shea, muscat rose bush or carrot) will give a cleansing cream or a base cream for dry skins.

Bath time

∽ Depending on where you live, your tap water may be too hard. To soften it, add vinegar cleansing lotion, or bran or oats, in a handkerchief or muslin bag.

∽ Our grandmothers loved to use benzoin dye to perfume and soften the water. You can buy it from pharmacies and you need only a few drops for the water to turn a delicate opalescent hue and release a lovely, slightly amber, scent.

∽ The best and most economical way to soften water and to obtain really soft skin is to add a handful of bicarbonate of soda to your bath.

∽ When you feel very tired and tense, add a fistful of coarse sea salt to the bath water. When rinsed and dry, clothe yourself in a soft nightgown and go straight to bed.

Vinegar cleansing lotion

This vinegar cleansing lotion is extremely easy to make; it neutralizes water hardness and at the same time leaves skin and hair soft and silky. Use a mixture of aromatic plants or choose a single one.

1L (1¾PT) CIDER VINEGAR

1 GENEROUS HANDFUL OF AROMATIC

PLANTS SUCH AS LAVENDER,

ROSEMARY, FENNEL, VERVAIN,

LEMONBALM, SANTOLINA, ROSE,

CARNATION, JASMINE, EUCALYPTUS

AND MYRRH

1. Heat the vinegar. When it starts to boil, add the plants and turn off the heat.
2. Pour into a stoneware jar or pot and leave to marinate for at least 15 days.
3. Filter through a coffee filter or a muslin-lined sieve to remove the impurities, then bottle.

Half a glass is enough for one bath.

This scented vinegar is also excellent as a softener for delicate clothes.

RIGHT-HAND PAGE
Vinegar cleansing lotion is made with cider vinegar to which have been added all sorts of fragrant plants such as lavender, rosemary, fennel, thyme and eucalyptus.

According to legend or tradition, the Empress Poppaea, Nero's wife, used to maintain the beauty and youth of her skin by taking a daily bath in milk. Today we know that lactic acid is excellent for the skin, but it is difficult and hardly practical to envisage copying Poppaea's example. However, we can use it as inspiration, and add milk to the bath water. Use powdered milk, with which it is easy to mix a few drops of essential oil or your favorite perfume.

You can also give a milky look to your bath water by dropping in a carefully knotted handkerchief, filled with skin-softening starch or cornflour, or by adding five or six drops of benzoin, which has a vanilla and balsamic scent.

Bran bath

A HANDKERCHIEF OR A THIN

GAUZE SQUARE

300–400G (11–14OZ) BRAN

OR OAT FLAKES

1. Fill the handkerchief or gauze with bran (found in a chemist's or health food shops) or oat flakes.

2. Tie all four corners together to secure.

3. Leave this sachet to soak in the bath water, until it turns milky.

You can also use this sachet to rub on slightly rough skin to smooth it, for example on the elbows, knees or heels.

Quince for irritated skin

Quince pips contain mucilage (a type of water-soluble gum), which softens the skin. Just leave them to soak in water. After having soaked for a few days, a translucent jelly will have formed which you can use to clean your face.

You can also obtain good results by mixing 25g (1oz) of quince pips with a glass of distilled water. Apply the filtered liquid as a soothing and restorative lotion for the face.

Quince water

50G (2OZ) QUINCE PIPS

50G (2OZ) FRESHLY PEELED

QUINCE BARK

1L (1¾PT) WATER

PINCH OF SALICYLIC ACID

1. Heat the water in a pan and, when it starts simmering, add the pips and bark.

2. Leave the liquid to simmer for 5 minutes then turn off the heat.

3. Filter the liquid and add the salicylic acid.

4. Bottle and keep in a cool place.

When Colette, the French writer, thought of becoming a beautician, she proposed, amongst other beauty products of her own invention, this water, named "Angel's skin", particularly designed for greasy skins.

RIGHT-HAND PAGE
Quince pips contain skin-softening properties. Leave them to soak in distilled water. This liquid once filtered can be used as a refreshing lotion for the face.

Officina Profumo-Farmaceutica

di S. M. Novella

firenze

Polver

✻ Iris Florentina

La Po...re d'Ireos va gelo...
...ll'umidità e da...inanza di qualunque
Se pr...qualunque perdesd...
...tempo, bene ste...
...le per fargl...

The properties of iris

༚ Once ground, Florence iris rhizomes make a fantastic natural toothpaste, which whitens and polishes teeth efficiently. Just dip a damp toothbrush into the powder.

༚ Florence irises are also used by perfumers as a fixer in some fragrances for they add a delightfully subtle note of violet.

Hair

༚ Always rinse your hair with cold water, and use vinegar or lemon juice during the last rinse to give it extra shine.

༚ Adopt the habit of adding beer yeast to your food. In powder or in tablet form, this product, rich in amino acids, promotes hair and nail growth.

༚ Beat two eggs with a tablespoon of rum: this was our grandmothers' favorite recipe for fortifying hair. Use warm water for this shampoo; if the water is too hot, the egg whites will coagulate.

༚ Panama wood water (see old-fashioned soapwort water, page 102) is an excellent shampoo for delicate hair, and is especially good for greasy hair.

Hands

༚ If you have to do dirty work, rub your nails with dry soap first. Your work is done, all you will have to do is brush your nails and they will be spotless.

Feet

༚ To soothe your feet, soak them in very hot water with a solution of coarse sea salt.

Lila's lemon and clove shampoo

1L (1¾PT) WATER

4 LEMONS CUT INTO QUARTERS

16 CLOVES

1. Heat the water in a pan and add the cut lemons and cloves.
2. Simmer for about 15 minutes, or until the lemons have turned into a sort of marmalade.
2. Filter and leave to cool.
4. Wet your hair, wring it out slightly and then apply the lemon purée. Massage the scalp and leave the shampoo to take effect for a few minutes before rinsing.

This amazing lemon concoction leaves your hair shiny, silky and nicely scented. It is particularly effective for greasy hair or alternatively for a very dry, scaly scalp.

Nail fortifier

OLIVE OIL

LEMON JUICE

COLOURLESS IODIZED ALCOHOL,

ALL IN EQUAL QUANTITIES

1. Mix all the ingredients together.
2. Warm slightly in a bain-marie. Store the mixture in a jar and dip your nails in it regularly.

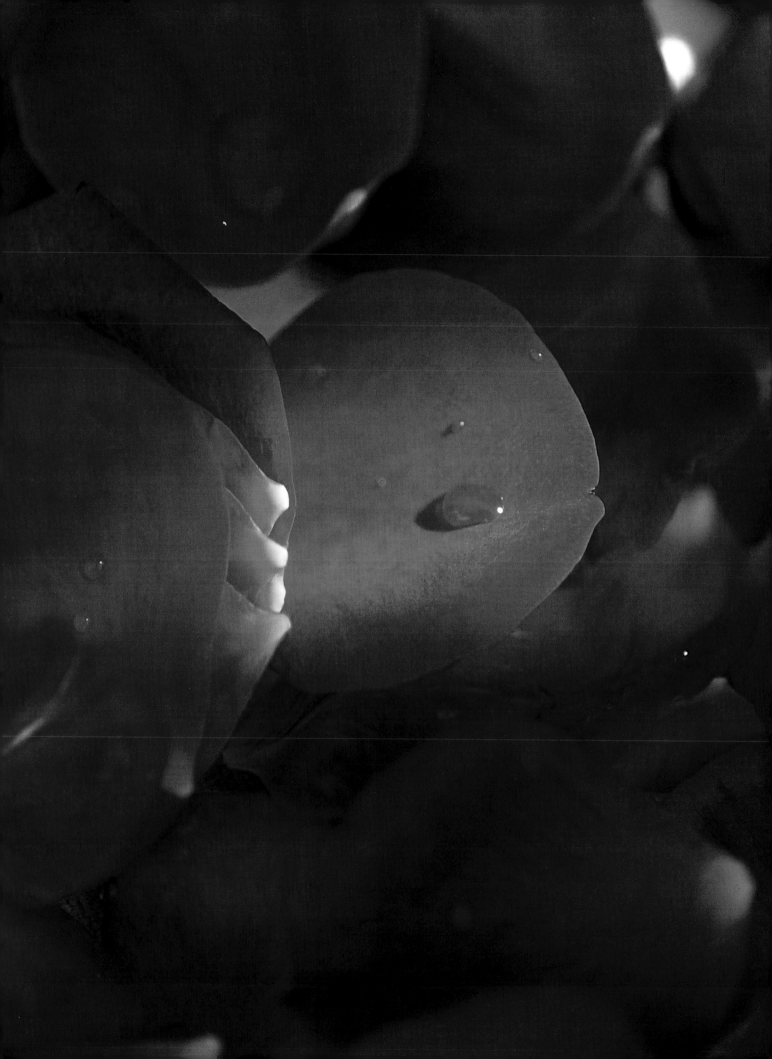

Perfumes and lotions

∾ Our grandmothers found time at home to prepare the creams and elixirs that were part of their beauty routine. Flower waters made from rose, witch hazel, elder or cornflower contained similar properties to our modern toners and left a delicate natural scent on the skin. ∾

Perfumes and scented waters

∾ You can enhance your perfumes or toilet water by adding spices such as cinnamon, pepper, cardamom or vanilla, which you can infuse. Be careful, these spices are better for "hot" and sylvan perfumes than for flowering green ones.

Rose water

500G (1¼LB) DAMASK ROSE
(CENTIFOLIA) PETALS

1L (1¾PT) DISTILLED WATER

1. Bring the water to the boil. Once boiling, turn off the heat and add the rose petals to the pan.
2. Leave to infuse for about 3 to 4 days, then filter the liquid.
3. Bottle the liquid, label and keep in the fridge. Unlike the true rose water obtained through distillation, this water does not keep for long and must be kept in the fridge. It can also be used as a toner after cleansing.

Facial lotion

5G (1⅙OZ) GROUND ALMONDS

2L (3¼PT) ORANGE FLOWER WATER

2L (3¼PT) ROSE WATER

5 DROPS BENZOIN DYE

1. Mix all the ingredients together, then bottle.
2. Leave to marinate for 15 days.
3. Strain through a coffee filter-paper or piece of butter muslin, then bottle again and label.
Use this lotion, specially formulated for greasy skin, as a toner after cleansing.

LEFT-HAND PAGE
Born in water like Venus, the beautifully colored rose has many positive qualities as well as beauty. Rose water is a lovely way to clean the skin.

Sage water

1 HANDFUL OF FRESHLY PICKED

SAGE LEAVES

500ML (16FL OZ) DISTILLED WATER

1. Chop the sage leaves very finely. Bring the water to the boil and add the herbs.
2. Turn off the heat and leave to infuse, covered, for 1 hour.
3. Filter, bottle and label.

This peppery and balsamic water can also be used as a facial toner (for skins that tend to be greasy, for example) or to massage the scalp. It also soothes sunburnt skin. Additionally, when used in a steam iron this sage water can be used to perfume clothes.

Iris water

250ML (18FL OZ) SURGICAL SPIRIT

25G (1OZ) GROUND FLORENCE IRIS

AVAILABLE FROM HERBALISTS

50G (2OZ) BENZOIN DYE

1. Leave the ground iris to marinate in the spirit for 1 week.
2. Filter, then add the benzoin dye.

You can add 10 drops of violet essential oil to give this iris water a stronger perfume.

Millefiori or Thousand Flowers water

1L (1¾PT) SURGICAL SPIRIT

400ML (14FL OZ) ORANGE FLOWER WATER

12.5ML (2½TSP) BERGAMOT OIL

5ML (1TSP) PERU BALSAM

5ML (1TSP) CLOVE OIL

1.5ML (¼TSP) NEROLI OIL

1.5ML (¼TSP) THYME OIL

1. Add all the ingredients to the surgical spirit and mix well.
2. Filter, bottle and label.

The old recipe for this flower water included 12.5ml (2½tsp) of musk oil, but this product, used as a fixer in the past, is no longer available (it is banned, because it was extracted from the anal pocket of certain animals, such as the civet, now a protected species). You could replace animal musk with plant musk, if you can buy it from a herbalist, or with synthetic musk. All the ingredients used here can be found in a drug store.

RIGHT-HAND PAGE
A few vanilla pods split in two will impart their warm and heady perfume to a simple amber-scented cologne.

BACK TO
nature

*O*f those who have the gift of making everything in the garden grow, popular wisdom says that they have "green fingers". Part magician, part alchemist, gardeners of times past knew the soil and its strange connections with the moon, as well as the art of combining or keeping apart particular plants.

For their gardens they developed techniques and concocted recipes that still retain their power today. The art of grafting, cutting or sowing was transmitted from father to son or mother to daughter. The vegetable patch and orchard were usually masculine territories, whereas the flower garden seemed to be the natural domain of women, where they gathered the components to decorate their bouquets.

Roses and rosebushes

*"Gardeners of our lives, in as much as we love, so we all have and all love
an exquisite memory of the rose."*

Denise Le Dantec, Le Journal des Roses (The Rose Journal*), François Bournin, 1991.*

*Cultivated granddaughter of the five-petalled wild rose, the rose has graced our gardens
since time began. The object of the gardener's every affection, every attention, it is the most
beautiful adornment in May and June, and sometimes consents to blossom during the first
frosts, like an ultimate offering before winter.*

The color of the rose

According to a Greek legend, all roses were originally
white, but one day Venus pricked herself on a rose
thorn and her blood colored the petals incarnadine
which has been their color ever since.

Traditional recipes

In the past, gardeners often used cooper-
sulphate-based Bordeaux mixture for their rose bushes;
it is also used to treat vines. Incidentally, this mixture
can be used to color a lovely blue-green new fence
or wooden trellis that look too new.

Some gardeners always buried garlic cloves at the
root of rose bushes. They said that it enhanced their
color and scent, while keeping the greenflies at bay.
As this treatment is harmless and does not create a
garlic aroma in the rose bed or garden, it can still be
practised today.

Climbing roses

When an old tree gradually loses its leaves but
keeps its noble shape, why not turn it into a support
for a climbing rose, which will give it back its youth.
Simply plant a rosebush at its base then prune the rose
so its stems will climb harmoniously into the old tree.

LEFT-HAND PAGE
*According to tradition garlic
cloves planted at the foot of a
rosebush will help improve
its vigor and scent while
protecting it from greenflies,
maybe because of the sulphur
they contain.*

ABOVE
*An old rosebush spreads itself
above a bench made
of branches, created by
Bruno Lafforgue in his garden,
at the Mas de l'Ange, a
farmhouse and bed and
breakfast in Provence.*

Old-fashioned frames for cuttings

In the past, to be sure that their cuttings would take, gardeners would place them inside frames made of long wooden boxes with a sloped glass top: basically miniature greenhouses.

∿ You can replace this old-fashioned frame by a simpler installation: use a large wooden box (a wine case for example) with, at the bottom, a thick layer of grass cuttings to replace the manure used by our grandparents, which generated a soft and beneficial heat that helped plants to grow. Grass cuttings will have the same effect but will smell less pungently than manure! Put your pots in the box, and cover with a sheet of glass or plastic to protect them and keep in the humidity.

Old-fashioned rosebush cutting

1 ROSE STEM TO REPLANT, WITHOUT FLO-
WERS OR BUDS

1 GRAIN OF WHEAT PICKED IN SUMMER
FROM A RIPE EAR OF WHEAT

1. Choose a stem that is still green and does not yet have a woody appearance.
2. Take off all the leaves found at the lower end of the stem and cut the stem to a length of 10cm (4 in) maximum.
3. Cut a cross at the end of the stem with a sharp knife and push the wheat grain into the cut.
4. Put the cutting in a glass of water overnight.
5. The following day, plant the stem in a small pot filled with ⅔ compost and ⅓ sand. Some traditional gardeners swear by this method, especially if you do this at the end of August or beginning of September: the best time, according to tradition. Strangely, some gardeners have noticed that rose cuttings planted at the edge of an earthenware pot grow better than those planted in the center probably because the heat is more intense at that particular spot.

LEFT
Copper-based Bordeaux mixture, sprayed on this rosebush to protect it, inadvertently gave an amazing color to the wall.

RIGHT-HAND PAGE
An old cherry tree is used as a support for the climbing rose; flowers, fruits and leaves thus intertwine beautifully.

Sowing and repotting

*"During its waxing or new phase, the moon promotes the growth of plants upwards and
the proliferation of anything that grows above the ground.
In its waning phase, it impedes these growth movements but helps anything
underground to flourish."*

Maison Rustique des Dames (Ladies' Rustic House).

∾ *Gardeners of old preserved their secrets and know-how in certain traditions, rooted as
much in common sense as in superstition or magic. This structured the times when sowing
and planting took place, taking account of the phases of the moon.*∾

Sowing with the moon

During the waxing phase of the moon it was usual
to sow flowers and seeds that should come out of
the ground and grow towards the sky, whereas during
the waning phase of the moon everything that needed
strong root systems or that was grown for the roots
was sewn or planted (potatoes, radishes, tomatoes,
cucumbers, gherkins, cabbages or salads, as well as
fruit). Even today some gardeners will never sow a
lettuce during a full moon, lest it should bolt and
run to seed....

Preserving seeds

∾ Keep your packets and seeds in a dry place, out
of reach of rodents or insects, by storing them in
airtight boxes or jars.

∾ If you gather your own seeds from your garden,
keep them in carefully labelled small bags, with the
name of the individual plant as well as the month
and year of the harvest. Old seeds that do not sprout
must be thrown away.

∾ Very small seeds should be covered with just a
few millimetres of earth, so as not to be suffocated.

LEFT-HAND PAGE
*It is important to label
plants carefully, making
them easier to identify
especially when you
are taking cuttings.*

ABOVE
*Enclosed in a jar, seeds are
protected from humidity. In a
glass of water seeds have been
left to soak so that they will
germinate.*

143

Seeds and sowing

∾ Some seeds are thick and slightly hard, those of sweetpeas, for example; if you soak them overnight in a glass of water before planting, they will soften and sprout more easily. If they are exceptionally hard, soak them in boiling water. You can also keep them in damp sand for a few weeks before sowing.

∾ Thicker seeds can be scratched with a file, which will help them to sprout more easily.

∾ On the other hand, when seeds are very thin it is best to mix them with sand, to obtain a better seedbed that will also be easier to thin out (that is to remove sprouts that are too close to each other and keep only the sturdiest and most vigorous). A good mixture to use in the seed trays is two thirds compost to one third sand, which is not too thin and not too thick. Do not push the seeds in too deeply, and cover them with just a thin layer of earth. To water them gently, it is best to use a spray, which will not move disturb the seeds.

Careful labelling

∾ If you are an enthusiastic gardener and are acclimatizing annual or unusual perennials, don't forget to label your plants. You will then know exactly where you have planted them (and you won't mow or dig where you shouldn't!).

∾ To protect your labels from the rain and sun, which discolour them, smear candlewax or a block of solid paraffin over the whole surface: the wax will make them weatherproof.

∾ If you can, buy copper labels, on which you simply write the name of the plant with a ballpoint pen to carve the metal indelibly. With time, the metal will acquire a lovely sheen.

∾ You can also make your own labels from a fine sheet of copper, (bought at a specialist shop), that you can cut to the required size.

ABOVE
Seed trays, cuttings ready to be planted and rooting powder in which cutting stems are dipped to help establish them.

RIGHT-HAND PAGE
Keeping a basket for small gardening tools and accessories means they will not be lost and will always be to hand.

Protecting plants

❧ *In the garden there are many dangers that threaten plants, including cold, excessive heat, insects and fungi. Using a mixture of magic and alchemy gardeners of times past concocted amazing recipes and knew how to combine plants so they could offer each other mutual protection.* ❧

Partners, or not

❧ Do not plant cucumber and melon seeds next to each other, as the latter will take on the bland taste of the former and lose all its sweet flavor...

❧ The same applies to marrows according to popular belief: "For a long time, it was thought that marrows grown near melon fields altered the taste of the melons. As a result, in Alpes-de-Haute-Provence it is still usual for someone who has purchased a substandard melon to estimate the distance that would have separated his melon from a neighboring marrow field. The less good the melon, the shorter was the distance: ten feet, five, two... and, in the worst cases, only a few inches."

Jean-Baptiste de Vilmorin, *Le Jardin des Hommes* (*The Men's Garden*), Le Pré aux Clercs, 1996.

❧ Cucumbers, however, thrive among peas, beans, radishes and sunflowers.

❧ Plant achilleas or nasturtium in your vegetable patch. Powerful-smelling achilleas keep insects away, and a shiny nasturtium bush will attract greenflies from the surrounding area, keeping them away from neighboring plants for a while.

Beneficial alliances

❧ Asparagus plants will protect tomatoes from disease when they are grown nearby, thanks to a substance that they contain called asparagine.

❧ African marigold, with its powerful and distinctive smell, should be included in all vegetable patches, as its scented roots keep away nematodes, which are worms that are as harmful to vegetables as they are to humans, whom they can infect.

❧ If you have apple trees in your orchard or garden, spray them regularly with shallot juice, as its powerful sulphurous smell wards off destructive insects. Alternatively simply plant a few shallots around the base of the trees.

Anti-greenfly potion

1L (1¾PT) WATER

115G (4OZ) LIQUID BLACK SOAP OR

SOAP FLAKES (GRATE SOME

HOUSEHOLD SOAP)

2 GARLIC CLOVES, CRUSHED

Mix all the ingredients and pour into a sprayer.

Anti-greenfly nicotine

50G (2OZ) PURE TOBACCO

1L (1¾PT) WATER

1. Leave the tobacco to marinate in the water for several days.

2. Dilute this solution: a capful of nicotine solution to 1l (1¾pt) water.

3. Spray on the areas invaded by greenflies.

This recipe is a long established one used to deter greenfly. It is efficient but should be handled with great care because nicotine is a violent poison. The liquid must be poured into a carefully labelled bottle and MUST be kept out of reach of children and animals.

Protection against the cold

If you have a fern in your garden, cut its fronds in autumn: These fronds will form an efficient protective straw against the cold. Just lay them thickly at the foot of plants to protect them. You can also cut fern fronds from other sources, such as woodland.

Widely used in the past by gardeners, glass bell-jars provided a good protection for the most delicate plants against cold winds and wintry frosts. Nowadays, they are sold in antiques shops, but some glass specialists make reproductions. You can also find plastic bells in garden centres, which are just as effective but not as decorative.

In the house or in the greenhouse, to activate the growth of your cuttings and seeds, you can use upturned glasses or transparent cheese-bells, which will work just like mini-greenhouses.

Snow itself protects plants naturally against the cold. Jean-Baptiste de Vilmorin, in his book *Le Jardin des Hommes* (*The Men's Garden*), quotes the example of a botanist who, during the terrible winter of 1937–38, recorded a temperature of 20°F (6°C) under 3ft (1m) of snow, when the outside temperature was 27°F (-33°C)!

On the other hand, ice is very dangerous to plants as it burns them and, if thick, it can snap tree branches. Remove any ice you discover.

ABOVE
An old glass bell-jar protects plants from both cold and dry weather. In summer, be careful that the sun does not burn the leaves behind the glass.

RIGHT-HAND PAGE
At the Château de Giniac, the most delicate plants are brought inside to the ground floor before winter, as in the orangeries of the past.

Protection against hot and dry weather

∾ Putting straw on vegetables protects them against hot and dry weather. In summer use grass cuttings for the same purpose.

∾ An old saying maintains that "one hoeing is better than two waterings" and this is quite true and a good tip to follow: soil that is regularly hoed dries less and retains its humidity longer.

∾ Tomato plants need plenty of watering. To water them more efficiently there is an old trick that gardeners use. Cut off the base of a plastic bottle and put the neck of the bottle in the ground at the base of the foot of each tomato plant. When you pour water into the bottle, it will spread into the earth slowly, directly to the roots of the plants.

∾ This method of cutting a bottle in half is also effective for watering certain moisture-loving potted plants that live on terraces and balconies.

Magical concoctions

∾ As soon as the weather gets warmer, greenflies invade rosebushes and other plants. If you do not want to use chemical treatments, try old traditional recipes made from black soap or household soap. The soap is dissolved in hot water at the ratio of one to ten. Some gardeners even add grated garlic cloves to these soapy mixtures to make them more effective.

Fortifying nettle tisane

500G (1¼LB) FRESHLY CUT

NETTLE LEAVES AND STEMS

5L (1⅛GAL) WATER

1. Place the nettle leaves in a bucket and cover with the water.
2. Leave the leaves to marinate for a few days before use. Use this liquid neat in a spray against greenflies, or diluted in spraying water. Nettles are rich in mineral salts and will therefore fortify the plants that are treated in this way.

The gardener's tools

❧ Is a good gardener recognized by his gardening implements? It is perhaps a moot point, but for them to be truly useful they must be kept in good condition, in exactly the same way as the garden that they are used to tend. ❧

❧ You can sand the wooden handles of tools so they are smoother to handle. To make them softer, smearing them with dry soap or a little paraffin is very effective.

❧ Put rakes away with great care, prongs against the ground, to avoid treading on them by mistake.

❧ To prevent tool blades from rusting, regularly wipe the metal with a cloth that has been dipped in petrol or motor oil.

❧ If you think you might lose your secateurs in the grass, choose a bright-colored pair, such as yellow or red: they will be easily visible, unlike green secateurs which can blend in with the grass.

❧ When a blade is rusty, rub the whole of its surface with the cut side of an onion sprinkled with sugar. Sweet onion juice will clean off the rust and stop it from taking hold again.

❧ Contrary to what you might think, shiny and beautiful stainless-steel tools are not always suited to the hardest tasks in the garden. Choose genuine tempered steel that will not twist or go out of shape when pressure is applied. Old tools can be picked up at village jumble sales or second-hand markets. Not only are they beautiful and have the potential to become collector's items, but using them will be a pleasure (as long as they are still in working condition). This is because the carved wood and shaped metal are designed as a result of centuries of accumulated knowledge, ensuring that tools were perfectly constructed for the hands that would use them.

❧ Gather all the gardening tools and accessories you need in one place. Introduce a system so that you put shears, dibbles, gloves, small rakes, propagators, labels, string and raffia in baskets or crates, so you won't have to keep looking for them.

Basic products to use at home

Simple and easy to use, the products which follow are tremendously versatile and have many other uses than those outlined in the previous chapters. They can be found in markets, supermarkets, hardware stores or drug stores.

Garlic

Usually used only in the kitchen, garlic juice is also a glue that has proven itself when repairing cracked or broken ceramic objects.

Garlic has been used since ancient times as a fortifier and thinner of blood.

If you want to lessen the smell after having eaten garlic, chew a few coffee grains, a clove, cardamom seed or try to get capsules of essential oil of parsley (available at pharmacies), which work extremely well and are a lot easier to carry around than raw parsley!

Methylated spirits

This is a product with many uses around the house: it can clean windows (when used with balls of newspaper) as well as electrical bulbs, the top of a cooker or the door of a fridge. It can even disinfect the telephone handset. When used with a soft bristle toothbrush, it can clean gold jewellery and give sparkle to precious stones (except pearls, coral and opals, which are too delicate to be cleaned in this way).

Bicarbonate of soda

In the kitchen, bicarbonate can replace baker's yeast when you have run out, and soften the water used to cook vegetables (potatoes, dried haricot beans, green beans, peas, split peas, lentils...).

Perfect for use as a multi-purpose cleaning product in every part of the house, just add a few drops of spirit vinegar or dish soap to the bicarbonate, ideal for cleaning both enamelled and plastic surfaces. It provides a good solution for disinfecting, deodorizing and cleaning the inside of the fridge. When washing woollens, add 2 or 3 tablespoonfuls to the rinsing water to soften it and even to get rid of the matting that forms on the surface.

As for beauty and cleansing, it gives shine to teeth when a wet toothbrush is dipped in it, and it softens hard bath water.

Spanish or Meudon white

These two names refer to the same product, which is still sold by traditional hardware stores. When diluted in methylated spirits, this white powder becomes more or less a liquid paste. It has been used through the centuries to make silverware and metal crockery, as well as glasses and mirrors, shine.

Lemon

If only a few drops are required, prick the lemon with a toothpick, press it, then put the toothpick back in like a cork! To extract all of its juice without a lemon squeezer, cut it in half, push in a fork and turn it vigorously around in the pulp. If you use only half, the other half can be kept under a glass turned upside down on a saucer.

Lemon juice is good for flavoring plain tap water. Cut the lemon in half and push in cloves to keep flies away and perfume the inside of a cupboard. Combined with fine salt, this solution gives a slightly abrasive powder that cleans all enamelled surfaces. It makes copper or brass-based metal shine as well as marble (as long as you rinse thoroughly afterwards). A half-lemon also cleans a tea or coffee-stained sink, and gets rid of the lime that builds up around taps.

For bodycare and beauty, it softens the skin of your hands and whitens nails. It can also whiten teeth, but do not use it too often as it is acid and could attack the enamel in the long run.

Soda crystals

These are among those traditionally used products often now forgotten, but which can often be of great use. Add a few handfuls to the soaking water of very dirty laundry to get rid of grease and prewash it. They make glasses and tableware shine and also help to mop slightly dirty tile or wooden floors thoroughly.

Lavender oil

Around the house, this oil perfumes the air when added to a potpourri or burned in a diffusing ring set on a bulb. Add a few drops to polish to give it a lovely smell and keep insects away. Our grandmothers often used to apply some to the inside of their cupboards and wardrobes.

For cleansing, add some to the bath water (a few drops are enough) for a soothing aroma. Or dilute it in alcohol to rub on your body after a shower or excersise.

Glycerine

Much used in the past, glycerine has almost been forgotten nowadays but it can be very useful.

Simply rub a mirror or window (in the bathroom or kitchen for example) with a soft cloth lightly dampened with glycerine until all marks are gone; when treated in this way steam will not stick to the surface. In winter, this is an effective technique on car windscreens (inside and outside) and, moreover, glycerine will also stop frost forming on windows.

Glycerine is also useful for drying autumn leaves.

As for winter beauty treatments, a few drops in rose or witch-hazel water creates a softening beauty product that protects the skin against the cold, especially hand and facial skin that is exposed to the wind. When you run out of hairspray, put a few drops of glycerine in your hair to give it a slightly wet look and to fix waves in place.

Milk

Milk can be used as an improvised paper glue. It will work even better if it is mixed with flour. It can also be used to clean ivory, patent leather or rubber boots. Ink stains on fabric fade as long as you act quickly: soak the stained area in fresh or curdled milk and then rinse. It can also make an earthenware vase or pot waterproof.

For beauty, fresh milk can be used as an improvised cleanser, very soft to delicate or irritated skin. Its by-products, such as crème fraîche or yogurt, are also excellent natural products for the skin.

Soap

Soap can be used dry around the house to make a stubborn drawer slide or to soften the unvarnished wooden handle of a broom. Flaked and diluted in hot water, it will wash delicate textiles perfectly. Black soap (in liquid form and sold in hardware stores) can be used to mop mosaic or stone tiles.

Household soap proved its usefulness in skin care long ago, but some skin, too dry and delicate, cannot tolerate it. Some people use Oriental soaps instead of shampoo made with olive oil rather than laurel oil, but when doing this, it is effective to then rinse with vinegar to restore the shine that soap has a tendency to dull.

Salt

When cooking we sometimes use a little too much salt. You can tone down the saltiness of a hot sauce, stew or soup, by adding a raw potato to absorb the excess salt. A pinch of coarse salt added to the bottom of a pan or a grill will stop fat spitting. A pinch of fine salt helps to whisk egg whites stiffly.

Around the house, fine salt is used to clean copper and marble when added to vinegar or lemon juice. It can also clean the sole of a dirty iron. A few handfuls of coarse salt are enough to revive the flames of a dying wood fire.

Talcum powder

Around the house, sprinkle the powder on the springs of an armchair or mattress to stop them squeaking.

As part of your beauty routine, talcum powder can replace dry shampoo. After washing, dust some on your body with a powder puff or thick brush ensuring that you will stay fresh even in hot weather. Sprinkled inside shoes, it prevents irritations as a result of the contact of bare skin on leather or canvas.

If you do not have any talcum powder, you can substitute it with cornflour, perfumed with 2 or 3 drops of your favorite essential oil (rose, lavender, jasmine...)

Vinegar

For cooking, when using red or white wine vinegar, gourmets will flavor them with garlic, shallots, thyme or rosemary. If you prefer less sharp vinaigrettes, use cider vinegar, which is less acidic and goes marvellously well with crème fraîche when flavoring an endive, apple and nut salad... To deglaze sauces (so as to dissolve the caramelized juice of meat), sherry or balsamic vinegars add extra refinement. Vinegar can even improve potato or rice: a few drops in the cooking water and they stay firm and white. Add a small amount of vinegar to the water when poaching eggs; this ensures that the white of the egg coagulates perfectly.

Use spirit or white vinegar either to soften laundry rinsing water or to clean windows. It deodorizes the fridge (when cleaned with hot vinegar), revives the colors of fabrics and gives shine to copper when mixed with flour and salt.

For cleansing if you want to prepare scented vinegar it is best to used cider vinegar: its smell is less strong and it is softer on the skin.

To alleviate insect bites or sunburn problems, watered vinegar applied with a compress or cotton to a sting or a light sunburn will relieve the pain and burning sensation straight away.

RECIPE LIST

BEAUTY
Bran bath, 128
Facial lotion, 133
Iris water, 134
Lemon and clove shampoo, 131
Lily oil, 121
Millefiori or Thousand Flowers water, 134
Nail fortifier, 131
Old-fashioned soap, 125
Quince water, 128
Rose water, 133
Sage water, 134
St John's Wort oil, 122
Vinegar cleansing lotion, 126

COOKING
Basil sauce, 18
Bitter orange marmalade, 33
Café au lait, 42
Curdled milk or yogurt with dried fruit and honey, 42
Flattened apples and pears, 25

Garlic tourin, 22
Home-made cheese, 41
Instant shortcrust pastry, 47
Normandy fat, 34
Old-fashioned fried eggs, 37
Oven-dried tomatoes, 28
Plume cake, 48
Preserved lemons, 14
Preserving butter with salt, 38
Refreshening rancid butter, 38
Roquefort with port, 41

DECORATION AND CLEANING
Candle making, 62
Copper paste, 92
Digitalis infusion for bouquets, 74
Furniture wax, 79
Green pot-pourri, 68
Leaf drying, 76
Lime paint, 54
Milk paint, 53
Paste for gold wooden frames, 80
Returning the shine to glasses, bottles and pitchers, 86
Silverware paste, 92
Soap wax, 80
Stained-glass curtain, 58
Wooden floor wax, 80

GARDENING
Anti-greenfly concoction, 147
Anti-greenfly nicotine, 148
Fortifying nettle tisane, 151
Old-fashioned rosebush cutting, 140

CLOTHES AND LINEN
Anti-moth sachets, 112
Cleaning straw hats, 114
Home-made dye, 109
Ivy water, 102
Old-fashioned starch, 106
Old-fashioned soapwort water, 102
Taking care of patent leather, 114
Washing powder for very dirty clothes, 101

INDEX

Achillea, 147
African marigold, 147
Alum, 30
Aluminium pans, 91
Ammoniac, 92, 94, 109
Anemone, 74
Apples, 25
Apricots, 47
Artichokes, 17
Asparagus, 37, 147
Barigoule, 17
Basil, 18, 68
Baskets, 94
Bay (leaves), 14, 25, 28, 38
Beans, 17, 101, 147
Beeswax, 80
Bell-jars, 37, 148
Benzine, 117
Benzoin dye, 126, 128, 133, 134
Bergamot (oil), 125, 134
Bicarbonate of soda, 17, 38, 83, 126, 155
Bitter orange (oil), 68
Black soap, 80, 147, 151, 156
Bleach, 71, 79, 80
Bran, 102, 125, 128
Breadcrumbs, 41, 47, 117
Bronze, 91
Butter, 37, 41
Butter muslin, 60, 133

Cabbage, 38, 94, 143
Cakes, 47–48
Camphor, 112
Candied fruit, 30, 47
Candles, 62, 67
Caramel, 48
Cardamom, 34, 156, 133
Carnations, 126
Carrots, 18, 126
Cauliflower, 14
Celery, 34
Cheese, 37, 41
Chillies, 14, 34
China, 86
Chives, 18
Christmas rose (hellebore), 71, 74
Cider vinegar, 126, 156
Cinnamon, 68, 121, 133
Citrus fruits, 13, 67
Cloves, 34, 68, 121, 131, 134
Coffee grounds, 86,
Colette, 42, 128
Copper, 91–92
Copper sulphate, 139
Coriander, 18, 34
Cornflour, 105, 117, 128, 156
Crème brûlée, 48
Crème fraîche, 22, 41, 114, 156
Cucumbers, 143, 147

Cuddly toys, 117
Curcumin, 109
Curdled milk, 41, 42, 156
Currants, 48
Curtains, 57-58
Cutlery, 83
Cuttings, 140, 148
Dahlias, 71
Digitalis, 74
Dried apricots, 42, 47
Dried flowers, 74–76
Dried fruit, 42, 47
Egg, 37, 126, 131
Eucalyptus, 126
Faience, 86
Fennel, 126
Fern, 148
Figs, 25, 28
Fish, 22, 83
Flax oil, 114, 117
Florence iris, 102, 105, 131, 134
Flowers, 71–74
Forsythia, 74
Frame for cuttings, 140
Fruit storeroom, 25
Furniture, 79
Gallnut, 109
Garlic, 14, 18, 20, 22, 34, 89, 139, 147, 151, 155

Gherkins, 34, 143
Glassware, 86
Gloves, 117
Glycerine, 76, 79, 94, 117, 155
Grapes, 14, 28
Greenfly, 147
Gum arabic, 106
Hair, 131, 156
Half-curtains, 60
Hats, 112,114
Hellebore (Christmas rose), 71, 74
Herbs, 18, 34, 41, 68
Honey, 42, 121, 122, 126
Horsetail, 89
Household soap, 79, 80, 94, 101, 105,
    125, 147, 151, 156
Hydrogen peroxide, 101, 105
Indigo, 106, 109
Iodized alchol, 131
Ironing, 106
Ivy, 102
Jam, 30, 33
Jasmine, 126
Jojoba, 126
Kitchen utensils, 89
Knives, 83
Labels, 86
Laundry, 101–106
Lavender, 111, 126
Lavender (essential oil), 68, 79 101, 105,
    155
Lavender (water), 105
Leeks, 34, 92
Lemon, 13, 14, 33, 67, 86, 91, 92,
    105–106, 109, 114, 122, 131, 155
Lemonbalm, 68, 126
Lemongrass, 68
Lilac, 74
Lime (paint), 54
Linen fabric, 57
Madder, 109
Madonna lily, 121
Marrows, 147
Melon, 13, 147
Methylated spirits, 91–92, 94, 105, 155
Milk, 28, 37, 41, 53, 54, 86, 89, 105,
    114, 128, 156
Milk jam, 42
Milk (paint), 53
Mint, 68, 121
Mirabelles, 14
Mirrors, 92, 94
Mosquitoes, 68
Moths, 111, 112
Muscat, 126
Musk, 125, 134
Myrrh, 125, 126
Nasturtium, 13, 147
Neroli, (oil), 68, 134

Newspapers, 86, 92
Nutmeg, 68
Oats, 126, 128
Olive oil, 17, 18, 22, 28, 83, 89, 122,
    131, 156
Onion, 20, 34, 54, 109, 122, 152
Oranges, 33, 67
Orange flower water, 105, 125, 126, 133,
    134
Oxalic acid, 105, 114, 105
Paint, 53–54
Panama wood, 101
Panama wood water, 131
Parmesan, 18
Parquet floors, 79
Parsley, 18, 34, 155
Pastry, 47
Patchouli roots, 111
Peaches, 47
Peach tree (leaves), 28
Pears, 25
Peas, 17, 147
Pepper, 111, 133
Perfumes, 133–134
Peru balsam, 134
Petroleum jelly, 114
Pewter, 91
Pine cones, 64
Plantain, 122
Plums, 14, 47
Poppies, 74
Port, 41
Potatoes, 91, 156, 143
Pot-pourri, 68
Pruina, 14
Prunes, 42, 47
Prunus, 74
Pyrethrum, 112
Quince, 67, 128
Radish, 143, 147
Raisins, 28, 42, 48
Repotting, 143
Resin, 121
Rhubarb, 38, 105
Room fragrances, 67
Roquefort, 41
Roses, 74, 126, 139
Rosebushes, 139, 140
Rose (oil), 125
Rose (water), 105, 105, 125, 133
Rosemary, 68, 112, 117, 126
Rosemary (essential oil), 101, 105
Rugs, 94
Rum, 48, 131
Saffron, 109
Sage, 68, 122, 134
Salicylic acid, 128
Salt, 14, 17, 18, 28, 37, 54, 62, 91,
    92,106, 126, 156

Santolina, 126
Saris, 58
Seed, 143
Shallots, 148
Shea oil, 126
Shoes, 112
Silk paper, 89, 111
Silverware, 91
Soapwort root, 102
Soda crystals, 80, 101, 155
Sorrel, 38, 92, 105
Sowing, 143–144
Spanish (Meudon) white, 91, 92, 94, 155
Stainless-steel pans, 91
Starch, 106
St John's Wort, 122
Strawberries, 14
Straw hat, 112
Straw mat, 94
Sunflower, 147
Surgical spirit, 134
Sweet almond oil, 121
Tableware, 89
Talcum powder, 117, 122, 156
Tarragon, 18, 34
Tarts, 47
Thyme, 17, 34, 42, 112, 121, 126
Tie-backs, 60
Tobacco, 111, 112, 148
Tomatoes, 28, 143, 151
Tourin, 22
Tripoli powder, 83
Tulips, 71, 74
Turpentine, 79, 80, 114
Vanilla, 48, 68, 133, 134
Vegetable preserves, 34
Velvet hat, 112
Vervain, 68, 105, 126
Viburnum, 74
Vinegar, 38, 54, 86, 101, 106, 109, 122,
    131, 155, 156
Violets, 71
Walnuts, 28
Vodka, 105
Wax, 25, 79,106, 112, 144
White pepper, 111, 112
Wicker, 94
Wild chrysanthemum, 111
Wild rose, 139
Wild thyme, 42, 112
Windows, 92, 94
Wine stains, 105
Witch hazel, 126, 133, 155
Wooden floors, 79
Wood fire, 64
Woollen clothes, 101, 112
Yogurt, 42, 126, 156
Zenana, 111

ACKNOWLEDGEMENTS

We wish to thank in particular Hélène and Bruno Lafforgue, of "Mas de l'Ange" in Molléges, Michèle Joubert of the Château de Giniac, Christine and Michel Guérard in Eugénie-les-Bains, Françoise and Pierre Gerin in Saint-Rémy-de-Provence and Mr and Mrs Bernard Lassus, who welcomed us into their home.

We also thank those who have helped and advised us during the writing of this book: Philippe Arnaud, Monique Herblot, Hélène Fournier-Guérin, Paul Jacquette, Muriel de Curel, Marie-Annick Louis and Maud de Rochefort; The Conran Shop, Blandine Le Roy, Christian Tortu and his team, Habitat, Fragonard, Au Nom de la Rose, Tsé & Tsé & Associates, Astier de Vilatte, La Puce à l'Oreille, Terre de Sienne, Liwan and Amin Kader.

ORIGINAL EDITION
Editorial Manager : Laurence Basset
Publisher : Matthieu Biberon
Creative Director : Sabine Büchsenschütz
Design : Michel Cortey

UK EDITION
Project Editor : Emma Clegg
Editorial Assistant : Lara McCann
Translator : Dominique Cook
Proofreaders : Rosie Hankin and Libbie Willis

Color origination by : PackÉdit, à Paris
Printed By : I.M.E., à Baume-les-Dames